Financial Tips for Teachers

Other books in this series include:

Travel Tips for Teachers by Sunni Bloyd

Acknowledgments for this Edition:

Terri A. Laurin, Certified Financial Planner
Nelson E. Owens Accounting Service, Enrolled Agent
The Palm Beach County (Florida) Bar Association,
    Jennifer Keating, Communications Director
Don Scholl, Certified Financial Planner

Financial Tips
for Teachers

Alan Jay Weiss
and
Larry Strauss

LOWELL HOUSE
Los Angeles

CONTEMPORARY BOOKS
Chicago

Library of Congress Cataloging-in-Publication Data is available:
LC Card Number 91-24407

Printed in the United States of America

10 9 8 7 6 5 4 3 2 1

First Edition (1990)
Second Edition (1990)
Third Edition (1991–1992)

Photograph of home on front cover courtesy of Kaufman and Broad Home Corporation. The text of this book, including opinions of authors, are not necessarily the opinions of Kaufman and Broad or any of its subsidiaries or employees.

Contents

Introduction:
Where Are You Now,
and Where Do You Want to Be?   9

    Where Are You Now?   9
    Where Do You Want to Be?   10
    This Book in a Nutshell   11

Part One: Planning for the Future   13

Chapter 1: Budgeting a Ten-Month Check
  for the Full Twelve   15

    The Teacher-Paycheck Savings Formula   16
    The Adverbs of the Savings Game:
      Where Is Easy, *How* Is Not   17
    Does Membership Really Have Its Privileges? 18
    Comparison Shopping on Larger Items
      Can Make a Difference   19
    Hope for the Best, but Prepare for the Worst—
      Find Out About Service and Warranties   20
    Automobiles: to Lease or Not to Lease?   22
    Never Lose Sight of Your Objective   25

Chapter 2: Savings—Your Greatest Investment   26

    Retirement Plans: the Early Bird Gets the Best Return   26
    Realizing a Comfortable—and Maybe an *Early*—
       Retirement Through a Tax-Sheltered Annuity (TSA)   27
    The Fixed Annuity   31
    The Variable Annuity   32
    Which TSA Is for You?   34
    The TSA Loan Provision   34
    Tips for TSA Shopping   36
    Additional Retirement Plans   37
    Don't Make Your Choice Alone   38
    Tips on Finding a Good Financial Adviser   39

Chapter 3: The Second-Biggest Investment—A House   41

    The First-Home Blues   41
    The Condo/Co-op Alternative   42
    Are You Cut Out for a Fixer-Upper?   42
    Are You Cut Out to Be a Landlord?   43
    Creative Funding   45
    Nobody Ever Said It Was Easy to Be a First-Time Buyer—
       or a Second-Time Buyer, or a Third-Time Buyer   45
       TSA Can Stand for "Temporary Stretching Apparatus"   46
    All Home Mortgages Were Not Created Equal   46
    Don't Shop for a Home Unarmed—
       Make Sure You're Pre-Approved   47
    Don't Shop for a Home Unaccompanied—
       Use a Real-Estate Broker   49
    Beware of the Interest-Rate Crystal Ball   49
    If You Can Pay Cash, Should You?   49

Chapter 4: Your Total Financial Picture   51

    If Growth Is Your Priority   52
    Saving Toward Your Children's Education   54
    If Investment Income Is Your Priority   55
    Your Money Is Worth Only What It Will Buy   56
    If It Sounds Too Good to Be True, It Almost Always Is   56
    Investing in Yourself   57

Chapter 5: A Smart Investment—
Paying Off Those Credit Cards   58

    An Equity Line of Credit May Be Your Answer   59
    If You Don't Own Property   59
    Bankruptcy Is *Not* the Free Ride It's Cracked Up to Be   60
    Alternatives to Credit Cards   60

Chapter 6: Protecting What You've Worked So Hard
to Accumulate   61

    The Cafeteria of Health-Care Benefit Plans   62
    You're Worth a Million   63
    You're Also Worth Thirty or Forty Thousand Per Year   64
    Insure Your Retirement in Case of Illness   64
    A Trio of Life Insurance Options   66
    Insuring Your Assets Without Hocking Them   68
    Do You Need an Umbrella?   69
    Jumping Ship Can Be Costly in the Long Run   69

Part Two: Increasing the Pie:
Tips for Supplementing Your Income   71

Chapter 7: Moonlighting—Making Extra Money
During the School Year   73

    One Skill All Teachers Have: Teaching   73
    Teachers Have a Way with Kids   75
    Teachers Work Well with People   76
    Virtually Anything Requiring a License or Certification
      Is a Potential Opportunity for a Teacher   77
    A Teacher's Specific Skills Can Translate into Extra Money   77
    Teachers Can Make Hobbies Pay for Themselves—
      and for a Lot of Other Things   79

Chapter 8: Teachers with Summer Jobs   83

    If You Already Moonlight During the School Year   83
    Teachers Can Make Summer Money Out in the Sun   84
    Working Abroad   84

Teachers Can Also Make Summer Bucks
    Without the Adventure   85

Part Three: Taxes and Legal Concerns   87

Chapter 9: Do You Need an Accountant or an Attorney?   91

    The Three Basic Varieties of Tax Assistance   92
    What About Legal Advice?   93

Chapter 10: Tax Tips Every Teacher Should Know   95

    The Nuts and Bolts of Income Tax   96
    The Many Faces of Income   96
    The Untouchables: Income That Is Nontaxable   97
    Trimming the Pie   99
    Itemization Does Not Always Add Up   104
    Trimming the Self-Employment Pie   105
    Don't Leave Withholding to the Whims of
        Your Payroll Department   110
    Project Your Self-Employment Income   111
    IRA and TSA Withdrawals: Know Your Options   111
    Another Reason to Estimate the Coming Year's Income:
        Planning Deductions   112
    Tips to Help You Avoid an Audit   112

Epilogue: Financial Planning Is Not Deprivation   115

    The Future Looks Bright—
        Save and Spend with Confidence   115
    Spend to Enjoy—You Deserve It   116

Where Are You Now, and Where Do You Want to Be?

WHERE ARE YOU NOW?

How much do *you* earn? The national average teacher's salary is around $30,000 per year (although some districts pay as much as $10,000 to $15,000 more than others, this diversity is often offset by comparable differences in the cost of living).

Just about everyone knows that teachers are underpaid, considering the required skills and talent, and the impact that teaching has on our society. Yet $30,000 per year, while low for professionals, does put teachers right around the national average income for all working Americans. Teachers can, and do, achieve their personal financial goals—but only if they use the tools available to them.

School districts and teachers' unions often don't tell teachers about these advantages, since it really isn't their place to give financial advice. As a result, all too many teachers are left unaware.

Hopefully, this book can be the beginning of an enlightenment.

Know Where You Stand

For a lot of teachers—for a lot of *people*—calculating their total net worth may seem depressing, especially if the answer is a negative number. So why bother? Because it is the only way to measure financial growth. You probably wouldn't make a cross-country drive without consulting signs and maps in order to know where you are along the way. Likewise, it is important to know where you are along the road to your financial goals, even if you're just starting out.

Calculate your net worth.

You can measure your current financial situation by adding up your assets (how much you have), then subtracting your debts (how much you owe). The result is your total net worth.

Common assets include bank accounts; checking accounts; stocks, bonds, and other investments; life-insurance cash values; annuities; and real estate (including a personal residence).

Common debts include educational, home-mortgage, automobile, and credit-card loans.

Ideally, a teacher's goal should be to retire on the *income* generated from his or her assets, thus preserving the principal. If you significantly deplete your assets during retirement, you may run into serious financial trouble.

WHERE DO YOU WANT TO BE?

Teachers are realistic.

Most teachers we've interviewed tend to have realistic and pragmatic aspirations. They are, therefore, usually well within reach. Goals—even of a strictly

- *Home ownership.* Do you see yourself owning your own home or other residential property?

- *College for children.* If you have children, or plan to, how much of a safety net do you wish to create against the rising cost of higher education?

- *Retirement age.* When do you want to retire? If it is difficult to think that far in advance, ask yourself how much longer you want to teach.

- *Retirement income.* How much money would you like to have accumulated by the time you retire? Or, more importantly, how much annual income will you want during your retirement years?

- *Retirement lifestyle.* Where do you want to live during your retirement years? In addition to staying in your own home, you may wish to consider a mobile home, a condominium, a rental apartment, or an adult congregate living facility (ACLF), such as a lifecare community, retirement community, or nursing home facility, if health problems occur.

financial nature—are a personal matter, and so there are no rights or wrongs, just preferences. There are, however, some important issues all teachers might consider when setting their financial goals. See the box.

While the answers to these questions depend entirely on the individual, everyone's answers will likely have one thing in common: the goals are probably all possible.

Teachers can and do own their own homes. Teachers can and do put their children through college. Teachers can, as we will show in these pages, potentially retire from teaching as early as age 55 and with as much as a half-million dollars or more accumulated in personal retirement funds, in addition to state pensions.

THIS BOOK
IN A NUTSHELL

Financial planning is an ever-changing game, but in these pages we will provide a basic understanding of the rules. In Part One, "Planning for the Future," we will take a look at financial planning and investments, home ownership, insurance, and ways to reduce existing debt.

Reading the tips and information presented here is no substitute for having an experienced professional look at your individual needs. Rather, the purpose of this book is to direct you to the right sources and to give you the kind of general understanding that can help you get the most out of those sources as you pursue your financial goals. Though every effort has been made to provide the most current and accurate information possible, you are strongly encouraged to consult with an independent, qualified financial representative or tax counselor before implementing any program.

Reach your personal financial goals.

Some teachers achieve their financial goals entirely within the teaching profession. Others supplement their incomes with moonlighting and summer jobs (which can sometimes turn into second careers). In Part Two, "Increasing the Pie: Tips for Supplementing Your Income," we will explore some of the ways in which teachers are able to supplement their incomes.

In Part Three, "Taxes," we'll be taking a look at some tax breaks that are available to educators.

Our aim is not only to enable you to maximize your financial potential—through your own insights, along with the advice of an expert familiar with your financial picture. More importantly, we want to help you be able to achieve your *personal* goals.

Financial planning is, ultimately, about much more than dollars and cents, interest rates, and tax savings. It is about realizing a desired standard of living and maintaining that standard of living once you have achieved it.

Planning
for the Future

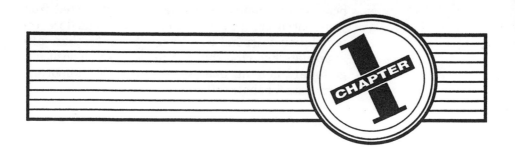

CHAPTER 1

Budgeting a Ten-Month Check for the Full Twelve

This section could also be called "How to Avoid Living on Credit Cards for Two Months." Yes, it would be a lot easier on many teachers if their districts spread their salaries over the full 52 weeks. Some districts will do this for you. For those of you whose districts won't, there are a couple of sane approaches to dealing with this situation.

The most logical way is to spread out the money yourself through automatic paycheck withdrawals, with the money deposited into a teacher credit-union savings account.

Teacher credit unions will usually pay a good market rate of interest on your money. In addition, *Use a credit union.*

because the money is automatically deducted from your paycheck, you gain convenience and lose the temptation to spend the money. Some teachers also appreciate knowing that the money they deposit will go toward helping finance cars and other important purchases for their colleagues.

THE TEACHER-PAYCHECK SAVINGS FORMULA

If you decide to use a teacher credit union to help spread out your 10-month paycheck over 12 months, the formula to use is simple. Just take one-sixth of your net* wages from each paycheck and have it deposited into your teacher credit union. At the end of the school year, you will have accumulated enough of a nest egg to maintain the same level of income during the summer.

Unless, of Course, You're in a High Tax Bracket

Some teachers in two-income households find themselves creeping into the upper tax bracket, and they may thus be better off putting their short-term savings into tax-free accounts that pay a lower rate of interest.

Are tax-free savings for you?

If, for example, you are in a 31% tax bracket, about one-third of your taxable income goes to Uncle Sam. If you put $5,000 in an account earning 8%, you would earn annual interest of $400 but net only $276 because of taxes. If you put the same $5,000 in a tax-free, money-market mutual-fund account earning only 6.5%, you would net $325. If, on the other hand, you're in a lower tax bracket—let's say 15%—then 8% taxable interest would net you $340.†

---

*The amount you use to calculate this should be your *net take-home pay,* not gross wages, since the teacher credit union is not a tax-deferred plan (which means that deposits are *not* tax-deductible, and interest is taxable).

†Since the above figures use hypothetical interest and tax rates, you would need an accountant—or at least a calculator and some current figures—in order to determine which plan would be best for your short-term savings needs.

The availability of these tax-free savings plans varies from state to state. Currently available in California, for example, are money-market mutual funds that give you complete access to your money and tax-free interest with a low minimum balance. A money-market mutual fund is one in which your deposits are used to purchase $1 shares in a portfolio of tax-free, short-term investments. The current rate of interest is determined by fluctuations in the interest rate on investments. There is generally no risk to the principal (the money you deposit). Further, many of these accounts are completely liquid. They allow you to write checks on your balance or remove your money at any time with no penalty if something better comes along.

THE ADVERBS OF THE SAVINGS GAME: *WHERE* IS EASY, *HOW* IS NOT

Of course, for many of us, the most arduous part of stretching income over the full year is not choosing the vehicle, it's gassing it up—in other words, spending less to save more. This is something with which virtually everyone must grapple at one time or another, if not *all* the time. So much to buy; so little disposable income.

So much to buy; so little disposable income.

Saving Money— a Function of Cash Flow

Most of your financial budgeting questions are not decided on a one-time basis. They are made every day and are measured in terms of your cash flow. A teacher was once asked about his cash-flow situation. He said it was in great shape: "The money flows in, and then it flows right out." That, of course, is *not* a great cash-flow situation.

Cash flow is the periodic (usually monthly) measurement of how much money comes in and how much goes out. A *positive cash flow* means that enough money comes in each month to take care of obligations and a little recreation, with some left over for savings. A *negative cash flow* means that too much month is left at the end of your money.

A negative cash flow means that too much month is left at the end of your money.

Saving Does Not Mean Starving

Those who are most successful at saving money are those who find the least painful ways of doing it.

There is no absolute formula for how to reduce expenditures. It's an individual process, involving a series of personal decisions geared to save money in ways that fit your lifestyle. Some teachers, for example, find that by dining out only infrequently they can achieve their savings goals, while others value restaurant meals enough to look elsewhere for savings. For some, the cost of commuting to work is so high that paying more to live closer to work can actually be a savings, others find that their financial goals can be met *only* if they are willing to spend an hour or two each day in a car on a highway in order to keep their housing costs down. Some teachers play the grocery-store coupon game and save hundreds of dollars a year; others would rather grow their own fruits and vegetables or belong to a food co-op. One factor, however, is almost universal: those who are most successful at saving money are those who find the least painful ways of doing it, but in a disciplined fashion.

DOES MEMBERSHIP REALLY HAVE ITS PRIVILEGES?

Membership stores are large warehouses that are part wholesale outlet, part retail store. They charge yearly fees (usually, around $25) and, sometimes, one-time joining fees. Membership stores sell items in bulk—for example, a six-pack of toothpaste—and so can offer prices well below those in supermarkets and drug stores. Many people, especially those with large families, save hundreds of dollars each year by shopping at membership stores.

For others, membership in such stores may not be advantageous. Anyone not saving at least $35 or $40 a year (or at least enough to exceed the yearly membership fee) would probably do better at the neighborhood market, thus avoiding a potentially long drive and the often endless lines.

Another factor is that some people tend to consume goods faster when those goods are more proximate. Such people are actually better off buying often and in small quantities, even at higher prices. For most of us, though, bulk is becoming part of economic survival. Thousands of American households are well stocked with tuna fish by the case, toilet paper by the tree. Bulk buyers may not realize it, but they are not only getting these goods at a discount, they are also fairly well prepared for a snowstorm, an earthquake, or a hurricane.

The Scientific Method

Since the initial financial investment is usually just a yearly membership fee and the potential savings are significant, a lot of people will use trial and error, trying out membership for a year to see whether they actually do save. A good way to measure relative savings is to comparison-shop your current supermarket with a nearby membership store and tally the difference. Don't forget to calculate the extra time you spend (or, in some cases, save) by going to a membership store.

Measure your potential savings.

COMPARISON SHOPPING ON LARGER ITEMS CAN MAKE A DIFFERENCE

Some discount warehouses also have good buys on expensive items, from typewriters and televisions to photocopiers. These, however, are not good items to buy on impulse. You can save considerably by comparing prices.

Many teachers on tight budgets not only shop around extensively but often postpone making large purchases of any items that are new on the market. New technology usually starts out expensive and gets cheaper as the months and years go by. Remember how much more computers and VCRs cost when they first came out? The prices of new items will generally level off in about two to five years—usually about the time the next generation of whatever it is comes on the market.

New technology usually starts out expensive and gets cheaper as the months and years go by.

Don't Forget to Read About That New Refrigerator

Smart shoppers do at least some research by reading consumer-magazine studies to compare what's available in, say, a washing machine, refrigerator, or cordless telephone. One problem with this approach is that by the time product reviews are in print, the particular models have sometimes already been replaced by new lines, with new numbers and features. However, research can at least give you a sense of which manufacturers are likely to give you the most for your money.

HOPE FOR THE BEST, BUT PREPARE FOR THE WORST—FIND OUT ABOUT SERVICE AND WARRANTIES

Even the most extensive research and testing cannot guarantee how long an appliance will endure. That's why it's always a good idea to investigate what kind of return policy and in-store service are available at a given store before you hand over your money.

The quality of postpurchase service varies to a large degree from store to store. Some stores, for example, will allow returns for virtually any reason with a complete refund within 30 days. Watch out for stores that levy a hefty "re-stocking fee" for non-defective merchandise you return.

Consumers Have a Bill of Rights— Find Out About Yours

Your implied warranty.

With the exception of Louisiana, every state has adopted its own variation of the Uniform Commercial Code (UCC), which grants a set of rights to anyone making a retail purchase. These rights are an *implied warranty,* meaning that when you put your money down for a product, you are entitled to certain reasonable assumptions. You should, for example, be able to assume that

- if a salesperson, merchant, or advertiser makes a promise, it is true (if you are told that a refrigerator is frost-free, for instance, you can assume that its insides will not turn into an iceberg); and

- the product will remain in working condition for a reasonable amount of time if operated in a reasonable manner.

How long this implied warranty lasts differs from state to state. A manufacturer's warranty may cover a product for only 30 or 90 days. Or it might not be a "warranty" at all, but rather a *disclaimer* of any liability for product defects. Such a disclaimer should not overrule whatever rights are granted to you by your state's law.

Should You Have to Pay for a Warranty?

In recent years, standard manufacturers' warranties on a great many products have decreased from a full year to 90 days. Part of the reason for this is that despite inflation, manufacturers are trying to keep their prices low. Limiting the length of product liability is a way to cut the product's cost without compromising its quality.

Are extended warranties really necessary? Do they always cover you for as long as the products work, and then just happen to expire simultaneously with the machines they are covering?

Actually, chances are that you will not need to exercise your extended warranty. That is why salespeople are paid a commission for selling them. These contracts are like insurance policies: if one, two, or even three out of ten warranty holders get free repairs, the store that writes the service contracts still makes a hefty profit.

Yet, still, if you can afford to extend the manufacturer's warranty, and if the peace of mind of knowing you will not be hit with repair expenses and anxieties is worth the added cost, you may want to give the extended warranty serious consideration. The

Pros and cons of extended warranties.

first thing to consider, these days, is whether the company offering you this service contract is reputable and solvent. In recent years, a number of companies have gone out of business, leaving contract holders in service limbo. Find out whether the service contract is with the retailer or with a third party. If it is with a third party, find out whether it's insured against bankruptcy. Some contracts will refund a percentage of the purchase price if the item is stolen (an important concern with regard to car audio equipment). Find out whether the warranty includes parts and labor for the duration of the agreement.

If you stand in the middle of a store and ask a salesperson all these questions, he or she probably isn't going to know all of the answers. You can, however, insist that written materials with all of these particulars be sent to you; then, if you so decide, you can probably cancel the contract and get a refund within a reasonable period of time.

Speaking of time, be sure to find out how long the manufacturer's warranty lasts. If someone offers you a "five-year" extended warranty, they aren't giving you five years on top of what you already get. The five years *includes* what the manufacturer gives you—so five years could be four years, and two years could be one year. *Know what you're paying for.*

AUTOMOBILES: TO LEASE OR NOT TO LEASE?

A teacher can avoid all of the headaches of automobile warranties and repairs by leasing a car—right?

Wrong. Leasing a car is not like leasing an apartment. Though the leasing company holds title to the vehicle, it is the responsibility of the lessee to perform all maintenance and repairs at his or her own expense. It is also the lessee's responsibility to put gas in the car, to wash it, and to insure it.

So what's the advantage of leasing, you may be

Budgeting a Ten-Month Check for the Full Twelve

asking? For some teachers, there is no advantage. For others, however, leasing may be a good option.

The Nuts and Bolts of Car Leases

A car-leasing agreement is a legal contract, and legal contracts are like snowflakes, all different (and anyone who tells you a contract is "standard" is speaking with a forked tongue). However, most car-leasing contracts are similar enough to describe in fairly general terms.

Anyone who tells you a contract is "standard" is speaking with a forked tongue.

The lessee picks out a car, just as a buyer does. But instead of the lessee's buying it, the *leasing company* buys it (unless the leasing company is a new-car dealer, in which case it already owns the car). With little or no money down, the lessee obtains the car by making monthly payments. These payments are usually less than monthly payments on an auto-purchase loan. The payments, in fact, are not based on a selling price plus interest, but on the selling price of the car versus the projected value when the lease is up (usually, five years). This is why leasing a Mercedes or BMW, which often depreciates at a slower rate than, say, a Cadillac, can be a bargain.

Once the lease is up, however, you are without a car. Most leasing companies will give you the option of buying the car at its current value. In other words, you can buy a used car knowing who has driven it, what kind of owner he or she has been, and what, if any, nagging problems there are with the car—and you can be sure that the odometer hasn't been illegally set back. If you don't like the way your car has been cared for, or if you're just tired of the same aluminum box, you can simply lease another car and continue making monthly payments. Some companies will let you change cars after two or three years without paying any more per month.

For a teacher with a sudden need for a car and with very little money for a down payment, leasing can be a way to get a car immediately. Too, some teachers find that they are comfortable paying $100, $200, or $300 per month in order to drive a late-model car (under warranty—meaning no major repair bills or repair-bill anxiety).

Not All Car-Lease Agreements Were Created Equal

Some car-lease contracts contain a clause requiring the lessee (you) to pay any difference between the leasing company's projected depreciation and the actual depreciation once the term of the lease is up. In other words, if the leasing company thinks the $10,000 car will be worth $4,500 after five years, but it turns out to be worth $2,500, you would owe the company $2,000.

Read the fine print. And remember the best advice of all: *There's no such thing as a standard contract!*

The Proverbial Financial Question: Is It Tax Deductible?

For most people, there is little or no tax advantage.

For some people, there are tax advantages with a car lease. For others, there are tax *dis*advantages. For most people, there is little if any difference tax-wise.

To begin with, you must be able to prove to the IRS that the car is used largely for business; if you cannot, there are no tax advantages to leasing. In the section on taxes, we will discuss the criteria under which you may deduct part or all of your automobile expenses. For now, here is the basic difference between deducting the expenses for a car you own versus a car you lease.

When you own a car, your deduction is a function of the car's depreciation. There are a number of ways to depreciate (or amortize) the car. The end result for all of them is that after a period of time—usually, five years—you have deducted all or part of the cost of the car (depending on how much you can prove you use the car for business). With a lease, the leasing company worries about depreciation. You simply deduct a percentage of the monthly leasing fee.

Is this less complicated than depreciating the car?

Yes.

Does it decrease your tax burden?

Not necessarily.

Only a qualified accountant or other financial expert looking at your specific set of circumstances can determine which situation will net you the greatest tax advantage.

No one ever said saving money was easy.

NEVER LOSE SIGHT OF YOUR OBJECTIVE

No one ever said saving money was easy. Even people who make enormous amounts of money can have trouble putting any of it aside. But the rewards of spending wisely are worth the necessary restraint of one's indulgences.

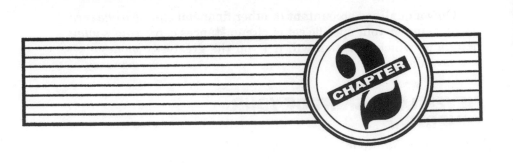

Savings— Your Greatest Investment

O nce you've mastered the cost of living, what are you going to do with all the money you'll save? Well, there are a number of needs just waiting to be satisfied. Retirement and a home top the lists of most teachers. Putting children through college and clearing away debt are not far behind.

RETIREMENT PLANS: THE EARLY BIRD GETS THE BEST RETURN

Each of us has a 55-, 60-, or 65-year-old person inside anticipating a comfortable and enjoyable retirement. That middle-aged self would probably appreciate it if he or she could have at least as much income during retirement as during the later working years, plus some kind of built-in protection for inflation. Since a pension will probably provide only 50–60% of the annual earnings in later working years, and since Social Security will not compensate for that additional 40–50%, you'll need to create other sources of income.

A pension will probably only provide 40 to 50 percent of your annual earnings.

How and where to invest your money are almost secondary to *when* you begin the process and to how disciplined you are at staying with the investment program. Because of the sheer number of deposits and the power of compound interest, an extra few years of investing—at the beginning or at the end— can virtually double your money.

This is not to diminish the importance of where the money is invested. Today, with the government eliminating many of our tax write-offs, there still remain two tax-deductible ways for most teachers to invest money that are safe, smart, and potentially very lucrative:

The sooner you start, the better.

1. the tax-sheltered annuity, and

2. the personal residence (not only something to save *toward,* but also a means of creating financial growth).

REALIZING A COMFORTABLE— AND MAYBE AN *EARLY*— RETIREMENT THROUGH A TAX-SHELTERED ANNUITY (TSA)

Beyond state teacher pension plans, there are only two types of tax-deferred retirement plans currently available to most salaried public-school teachers.* Teachers may contribute to an individual retirement account (IRA) or a tax-sheltered annuity (TSA).

Until the recent tax-reform law, anyone could contribute up to $2,000 annually to an IRA and deduct the full amount from net income. Now, however, the tax advantages have greatly diminished. A single

---

*Teachers with self-employment income or with working spouses may be eligible for other retirement plans, which will be addressed later in this chapter.

person who earns between \$25,000 and \$35,000 per year and who is covered by a retirement plan at work can take only a partial deduction; and this same single person earning more than \$35,000 cannot deduct any part of an IRA contribution. A married couple filing jointly may take the full IRA deduction only if their income does not exceed \$40,000 per year; if their income is more than \$50,000 per year, they may not deduct any part of an IRA contribution if *either* spouse is covered by a retirement plan at work. These changes in the tax laws have made the TSA the clear choice for teachers desiring financial growth toward their retirement.

The tax-sheltered annuity,* usually provided by life-insurance companies (and regulated by state insurance departments), allows teachers to deposit a much larger amount of tax-sheltered income. The exact amount is derived from an Internal Revenue Service formula based upon an individual's years of service, current salary, and prior contributions to retirement plans. For those with fewer than 15 years of service with their current employer (school district), the maximum amount of deferable compensation is \$9,500 per calendar year; for teachers who have 15 or more years of service with their current employer, the amount can go as high as \$12,500.

This savings tool was initially created by Congress for employees who did not participate in Social Security. These days, however, eligibility for a TSA is not restricted to such employees. Any employee of a public-school district or certain other nonprofit organizations (including some parochial schools) is currently eligible to enjoy the tax-deferred savings of the TSA.

You can now get competitive interest rates on a TSA. As of this writing we have seen rates of between 7% and 9%, and most will guarantee the interest not to drop below 4%. And remember, this is *tax-deferred* interest! You don't pay a dime of it to the IRS until you withdraw the money during retirement (at which time you will likely be in a lower tax bracket).

Current tax-sheltered annuity interest rates are

---

*The TSA should not be confused with a TDA (tax-*deferred* annuity), which defers taxes on interest only, not on deposits. Tax-deferred annuities are available to the public at large.

Savings—Your Greatest Investment

not guaranteed. However, since this is a long-term account, a fluctuating rate will tend to act as a protection against inflation. This is because the money you deposit into your TSA is reinvested by the insurance company in bonds and other assets that tend to be sensitive to the long-term ups and downs of interest rates and other indicators. This means that as certain interest-rate indicators fluctuate, so does the rate paid by your TSA. And since interest rates almost always increase in times of inflation, your savings growth can keep pace with any shrinkage in purchasing power. Keep an eye on the *actual* earnings you receive from those insurance companies which credit different interest rates on separate parts of your account, a process known as "banding."

The Nuts and Bolts of a TSA

With a tax-sheltered annuity, a teacher enters into an agreement with the school district to have a specific amount deducted from each paycheck and deposited in an annuity account. While the school district is not required by law to provide access to all companies offering TSAs, the IRS does provide guidelines that allow teachers a reasonable choice of tax-sheltered annuities. In other words, while a district may show favoritism to particular TSA providers, it may not prevent its employees from purchasing a TSA altogether.

A TSA contribution can be as little as $10, though some plans have a minimum of $50 or $100 per month. Aside from any minimum requirement, your monthly contributions should depend on your current cash-flow and tax-relief needs and on the time you have available to build up your retirement nest egg.

Contribute monthly.

Current law allows you to begin taking money out of your tax-sheltered annuity as early as age 55, if you are retired and receiving a pension (if applicable). If you keep working, TSA disbursements are allowed at age 59½ or later.* The only other three

---

*A recent IRS ruling waives the usual 10 percent penalty for plan withdrawals prior to age 59½ if the withdrawals are part of a series of "life expectancy" distributions. See your tax adviser for clarification.

conditions under which the monies from a TSA may be withdrawn are the death of the employee, total disability of the employee, or severe financial hardship, as defined by the IRS.

Though the principal and interest in a TSA accumulate tax-free during the account's growth phase, the money *is* taxable upon withdrawal. Because the government wants to collect taxes due, the IRS requires you to begin making systematic withdrawals no later than April 1 of the calendar year following the year you attain age 70½.

Each TSA plan has its own schedule of charges, most of which can be avoided by adhering to the guidelines of the plan. Otherwise, you may withdraw the money as fast as you want (depending, of course, on the length of your retirement and on your tax structure, since the money is taxable upon withdrawal), or you may withdraw the money as slowly as the IRS will allow.

Start Your Financial Clock Ticking

Many younger teachers begin their TSAs with modest monthly deposits, increasing those deposits as their salaries increase with tenure, promotions, and labor negotiations. Even teachers who simply cannot imagine ever being retired can easily imagine benefiting from the tax-sheltered annuity's loan provision (which will be explained later). Those who can imagine retirement, and who would like to make that retirement an early one, can set the wheels in motion toward that goal.

Retire early.

For example, if you opened a TSA at age 25 and contributed $400 per month for twelve months per year (not an uncommon teacher contribution) that's a savings of $4,800 per year. If you maintained a yearly contribution of $4,800 for the next 30 years, you could retire at 55 with slightly over $550,000.* Bear in mind that during those 30 years you would have contributed only $144,000. Yet because of discipline and time and compounding of tax-deferred earnings,

---

*This calculation is based on a hypothetical 8% rate of interest.

the amount contributed would have grown into quite a nice sum.

If, however, you were to wait until you were 30 before beginning the same TSA contributions, by age 55 you would have accumulated only about $360,000—roughly two-thirds of what you could have had with an additional five years. To achieve your financial goal, then, you would have to postpone retirement for an extra five years.

The amount of your monthly TSA deposits can be changed each calendar year. Also, within the rules of the particular TSA account, the deposits may be stopped and restarted periodically (for example, in the event of an emergency or of any temporary need for additional disposable income). But because of the tax-deferred nature of this account—that is, because it is not subject to current state, local, or federal income tax, on either principal or interest—such adjustments are not often necessary. Sometimes the TSA deposits from the monthly paycheck have little, if any, impact on take-home pay. Remember, what counts is not what you *make,* it's what you *keep.* By reducing your taxable income each month, you might slip into a lower bracket and not lose very much of your monthly cash allotment.

Remember, what counts is not what you make, *it's what you* keep.

If You've Seen One TSA, You *Haven't* Seen Them All

There are a number of factors that can vary from plan to plan, but in general terms, there are two kinds of tax-sheltered annuities: fixed and variable.

THE FIXED ANNUITY

A fixed TSA is a tax-deferred retirement plan in which the fund's investments affect the rate of interest but not the value of the accumulated capital. This means that the money you deposit each month is guaranteed by the company, as is the interest you accumulate. The word *fixed* does not apply here to the rate of interest, as it does in a fixed home-mortgage loan. In a fixed annuity, *fixed* applies to the safety of your principal. The only variable, in fact, is the interest rate.

If the TSA provider's investment portfolio does well, the interest will normally increase, and your money will make more money. If the investments do poorly, usually the worst that can happen is that your money will grow at a slower rate than it might have with a different TSA or different savings plan (usually, it is guaranteed not to go below 4%). But, again, since the investments in many TSA portfolios are interest-rate sensitive and fairly conservative, it isn't likely that your money will do any worse in your TSA during times of economic sluggishness than it would have in most other types of savings accounts.

In most states, a guaranty fund has been set up through legislation to pay benefits to fixed annuity policyholders whose insurance company has become insolvent. Check with your state insurance department to find out if your state has a fund, and if so, what it covers.

THE VARIABLE ANNUITY

If you are something of a gambler, you can invest toward your retirement with a variable TSA.* With this type of plan, your money may be invested in stocks, bonds, or other fluctuating investments. While you don't buy and sell actual shares of stocks and bonds, you often have a choice of which fund (stock fund, bond fund, or money-market fund) you want your money invested in at any given time in order to try and gain the maximum return. It's a little like playing Wall Street with tax-deferred dollars.

With a variable annuity, you take the risk.

There are usually substantial fees for such transactions,† but if you keep on top of these investments—and market trends—and have a lot of luck, you could accumulate a small fortune for your retirement. If, however, you are not a wise investor, or if you simply

---

*By "variable TSA," we mean a variable annuity or a mutual fund issued under sections 403(b) or 403(b)7 of the Internal Revenue Code.

†Such fees may include administrative charges, transaction fees, mortality charges, asset-management fees, and so on.

have bad luck, you could not only miss out on a competitive rate of return, you could lose part—or even all—of your personal retirement savings.

To put it another way, with a fixed TSA, the insurance company takes the risk; with a variable annuity, *you* take the risk.

Timing and Discipline Are Everything

With a variable TSA, much of your investment will tend to be relatively unstable. It will rise and fall pretty much along with the rest of the stock or bond markets. This means that the time to start a variable TSA is while markets are bearish (that is, when the average values of stocks and bonds are relatively low), and the time to have most of your accumulated savings in the account is during a bullish market (when values are booming).

If you do choose a speculative account, you need the intestinal fortitude to weather short-term depreciation of your account, knowing that in the long run—unless our economy goes into an uncontrollable tailspin—you may come out ahead. If you get impatient or panicky and pull out when things look bad, you can lose all of your hard-earned savings. Some protection against market fluctuations is inherent in the variable TSA, since money is invested regularly in like amounts (this is known as "dollar cost averaging"). This assumes, however, that you will never change your TSA deposit amount, temporarily stop contributing, or change your investment option—an unrealistic scenario.

Dollar-cost averaging.

If, however, you still think a variable TSA is for you, hedge your bets by not only using "dollar cost averaging," but also by liquidating your account at retirement using "systematic withdrawals." In other words, invest the same amount each month while you're working, and then withdraw a steady monthly income when you retire. Because mutual funds have generally fared better than insurance company managed accounts, try to select a variable plan offering a selection of options managed by well-regarded mutual fund families. To further manage these accounts, you may wish to use a "timing service" to oversee the

The Variable Annuity

movement of your account dollars in and out of the market. (Because these services charge up to 2½% annual fees—based on the increasing or decreasing value of your account—choose a timing service with a solid track record.)

WHICH TSA IS FOR YOU?

If you're not the type of person who would lose sleep over the state of your money in a potentially volatile market, and if you have other assets to backstop your retirement, you might benefit from a variable TSA.

However, most teachers will usually go with a fixed TSA. They might speculate a little here or there—through the stock market, the bond market, the state lottery, Las Vegas, or the track—but they'll do it with *after-tax dollars; not with their retirement savings.*

A lot depends on the fund manager. The risks of a variable TSA are not limited to those in financial markets. The success of any variable TSA account depends to a considerable degree on the knowledge and instincts of the person or persons managing the investments within each stock, bond, money market, or other fund. So while you might be very impressed with the current fund manager, you may discover a few years (or even a few months) after starting a variable account that that person has gone on to greener pastures. The new fund manager might be just as good, or even better—but then again, she or he might not be. You could, depending on the rules of the plan, possibly move your money elsewhere, but by doing so you might be pulling your money out at precisely the *wrong* moment with respect to the market.

Perhaps the most significant reason many teachers choose to stay away from the variable TSA is that it can lack the loan provision of the fixed TSA.

THE TSA LOAN PROVISION

Perhaps the greatest advantage of a fixed TSA over a variable TSA or an IRA is that you can usually borrow against it for *up to half of its current accumu-*

*lated value,** and for as reasonable a rate as 2% interest. If, for example, you've accumulated $30,000 in principal and interest after 5 years (which is about what you'd have with contributions of $400 per month), you could borrow as much as $15,000. This can be especially helpful for the first-time home buyer.

Although the interest from a TSA loan is no longer tax deductible, the potentially low interest rate usually keeps these loans an attractive option, especially when they're used to finance down payments on personal residences. In fact, all loans made against the TSA that are *not* for the purpose of purchasing a primary residence must be paid back monthly or quarterly in equal installments of principal and interest over a period of no more than 5 years, whereas those that are for this purpose may be amortized over a period that may be as long as 30 years.

The current "cost" of a TSA loan is about 10%. This cost consists of the loan interest rate charged, plus any loss of interest you incur on that portion of your account which serves as collateral for the loan.

"Paper" losses versus "out-of-pocket" losses.

TSA Does Not Stand for "Temporary Savings Account"

A five-year TSA loan can be used to help pay off past debts (especially those incurred at high credit-card interest rates) and to pay for any costly emergency needs (such as the sudden need to purchase four cross-country airplane tickets at upward of $1000 each). And you might want to use the loan provision for any sound investments that come along—investments that might make your money grow faster than if it is in your tax-sheltered annuity.

Pay off past debts.

But it's wise not to abuse the loan provision—and eradicate the long-term growth benefits of the TSA—by using the account to finance Christmas shopping, summer vacations, Las Vegas or Atlantic City weekends, lottery binges, or other short-term thrills.

---

*You may borrow against all of the first $10,000, per IRS rules, subject to individual insurance company guidelines.

TIPS FOR TSA SHOPPING

There are a wide range of rules and features among tax-sheltered annuity plans. A careful study of an assortment of plans, done with respect to your own financial needs, is advisable. Life-insurance companies offering tax-sheltered annuities are rated for safety by the A. M. Best Company (Oldwick, NJ). Look for an "A" or "A+" rating.

In addition, check with two other rating services to corroborate A. M. Best's findings: Standard & Poor's (New York, NY), whose top three categories of insurance company solvency for subscribing companies are "AAA," "AA+," and "AA;" or Weiss Research, Inc. (Palm Beach, FL), whose acceptable rating should be "B" or better.

Two Types of Fixed TSA's—Take Your Pick!

- "Single-tier" annuities have one interest rate. These TSA's stress maximum withdrawal flexibility and liquidity. They are best suited to the teacher who wishes to withdraw his or her funds on an intermittent or lump-sum basis after retirement (more and more, single-tier TSA's have become the annuity of choice.)

- "Two-Tier" annuities have a dual interest rate structure. These TSA's emphasize maximum accumulation of funds. They are best suited to the teacher who desires to retire with a consistent series of equal payments over his or her life expectancy, similar to payouts from a state teachers' retirement plan or social security.

Go into details on your potential TSA.

The next factor to consider is *where the life-insurance company offering the TSA has its money invested,* since this could determine the growth of your money over the next 25 or 30 years. Ask to see, in writing, a breakdown of what the provider is investing in. Look for safe investments, such as U.S. government securities and high-grade corporate bonds. (There is, of course, no way to know for sure how a set of investments will do, but you should at least feel that if you were in charge of the money you would invest it similarly.) Too much money in aggressive stocks, "junk bonds" (high-yield, low-rated issues), or "junk mortgages" can be a sign of potential trouble.

ADDITIONAL RETIREMENT PLANS

At the moment, the TSA is the best privately funded retirement plan for salaried public-school teachers. Depending on individual circumstances, however, some teachers may be eligible for additional retirement programs.

The 401(k) plan

This is a corporate employee-retirement plan, so if you do not have a spouse who works for an eligible company, you can skip this section. A number of teachers, however, do have spouses who may be able to take advantage of this plan. 401(k) plans can have competitive investment options that are tax-deferred, and they can often give eligible employees the additional choices of having retirement dollars invested tax-deferred in company stock, mutual funds, or other short- or long-term investments. Some 401(k)s have loan provisions similar to those of a tax-sheltered annuity. Some even have employer-matching bonuses, in which the company will match a portion—sometimes as much as 50% or more—of an employee's contributions.

Keogh and Simplified Employee Pension (SEP) Plans

If either you or your spouse has self-employment earnings, through your own business or through free-lance work, you may want to stash some savings in a Keogh or SEP retirement savings plan. Both are self-employment retirement programs allowing tax-deferred contributions and earnings. They can be set up through banks, savings and loans, brokerage houses, financial planners, or insurance agents. If self-employment income is derived from a business that has employees, be aware that both programs require that you include most employees in the retirement plan.

Save some of your self-employment income, tax free.

In general, SEP plans are simpler to set up and administer than are Keogh plans. For additional details, consult with your tax adviser to determine the best way to proceed. Of course, if your self-employment efforts turn out to be *big* business, and you decide to incorporate, you may be able to set up a pension, profit-sharing, or 401(k) plan of your own!

IRA Rollover

If you or your spouse has a 401(k) plan, and either of you changes jobs or stops a self-employed enterprise, you may want to consider rolling over any pension monies from a frozen 401(k), Keogh, or SEP account into an *IRA rollover* account. This can be done through a bank, savings and loan, brokerage house, financial planner, or insurance agent.

The IRA rollover is like the basic IRA account in terms of the rules of withdrawals and taxation (the money may be withdrawn any time after the attainment of age 59½, and it is taxed at the current rate with each withdrawal). However, unlike the simple IRA, the IRA rollover is a one-time movement of funds—within 60 days of the receipt of those funds—from any existing retirement plan to which contributions are no longer being made. Often, the IRA rollover offers more flexibility than a frozen pension.

Some companies offering 401(k)s may require you to withdraw the money if you are no longer working for them. If at that time you do not need the money and would rather continue to defer taxation on it, the IRA rollover is a good vehicle.

TSA Transfers

If the TSA plan or plans you own become unsuitable for your current needs, you may transfer part or all of your account(s) to another plan or plans, usually on a "tax-free exchange" basis. Before doing this, however, weigh any surrender charges you might incur, as well as the restrictions you will inherit with the new plan(s) you transfer to. Plan not to keep too much money in any one TSA account. *Diversify* your holdings.

DON'T MAKE YOUR CHOICE ALONE

Decisions and comparisons about retirement plans are best made with the guidance of an experienced financial counselor—someone who can analyze your financial situation, goals, and current cash-flow needs.

An experienced financial counselor can help analyze your needs.

Find someone who is well versed in the rules and particulars of retirement programs, and who can take all the numbers and formulas and translate them into dollars and cents (and sense) for you. Your financial adviser should also be able to look at your tax situation and figure out what will be most advantageous for you.

If you opt for a tax-sheltered annuity, a knowledgeable adviser can not only help you choose which TSA best suits you, he or she can also weed out questionable TSA accounts. A good adviser can also help determine a healthy structure of TSA deposits by looking at your current obligations and tax situation.

TIPS ON FINDING A GOOD FINANCIAL ADVISER

If you had a serious medical problem, you'd probably try to find the best doctor available. Likewise, if you were in serious legal trouble, you'd probably try to find the best lawyer you could. You should take the same approach to financial planning. You deserve the best. Your future is at stake, and you need to make certain you're in the right program.

You deserve the best.

A lot of teachers have bought tax-sheltered annuities or other investment plans from salesmen soliciting business in the school's faculty cafeteria. Some of these brokers may come highly qualified, but others could lack sufficient knowledge of taxes and other necessary variables. While most financial brokers know the catch phrases, not all of them know the important particulars of the various programs.

Unless you are absolutely sure you are being given the best, most useful advice, should you really take the chance on what may literally amount to your life's savings?

Before Listening to Financial Advice

Following are some important things to find out about a financial adviser before you spend your time or money.

Look for experience and trustworthiness.

- How long this person has been doing financial planning.*

- How large his or her organization is.

- Whether the person does financial planning as a *full-time* job (think twice before taking advice from someone doing it as a sideline to make extra money).

- What other teachers in your district he or she has done business with (for references).

- Whether he or she has a college degree.*

- Where he or she was trained.*

- Whether he or she represents more than one insurance company.

You can often avoid having to ask these questions directly if you let the referrals of respected coworkers guide you toward the right adviser.

Think twice about dealing with anyone who has less than one year's experience. If this sounds a bit harsh on those starting out, consider this: it is not uncommon for an inexperienced broker to change jobs within a year, or even a few months. To ensure that you will be able to get ongoing financial service as your needs change, deal only with a qualified professional.

No Company Bias, Please

You can't choose if you don't have a choice.

Find someone who works for an independent organization, with no direct ties to any company offering tax-sheltered annuities or other investments. Otherwise, you might not be given an objective assessment of the merits of the different plans available, and your adviser may push you toward a program that's not the best one for your individual needs. You can't pick the right retirement savings plan if you don't have a choice!

---

*A comprehensive résumé should answer these questions.

The Second-Biggest Investment— a House

You're never too young to buy your first home. With the help of a fixed tax-sheltered annuity and loan provision, the down payment may be more accessible than you think.

You're never too young to buy your first home.

Real estate can often appreciate over the course of a few years. And the interest on your home mortgage is—and hopefully always will be—tax deductible.

THE FIRST-HOME BLUES

Buying one's first personal residence can be a painstaking process. This is especially true in major urban areas, where real-estate prices are most volatile. There are, however, a number of ways that teachers can—and do—put themselves on the real-estate map. These include the purchase of condominiums and co-operatives, fixer-uppers, and owner-occupied rental property, along with creative approaches to raising down payments.

THE CONDO/CO-OP ALTERNATIVE

Usually, no personal real-estate investment is as advantageous as a house. But if financial restrictions or the high prices of homes where you live limit you to buying a condominium or co-op apartment—or if you'd just rather not have the headaches of a house to contend with—then buying an apartment unit or townhouse can be a good alternative.

The difference between condo and co-op.

The principal difference between a co-op and a condominium has to do with the legal aspects of ownership. With a co-op (also known as a stock co-operative), you do not actually own the apartment you live in; rather, you own shares of stock in the entire building or housing complex. Because you do not actually own the unit you are living in, it is more difficult to sell a co-op unit. Prospective buyers usually have a more difficult time financing the purchase. Also, prospective buyers must be approved by a co-op board. Another disincentive to owning a co-op is that shareholders must share any financial responsibility incurred if someone in the building defaults.

With a condominium, you own your unit, making it much easier to buy and sell. For this reason, the same apartment or townhouse is often worth more if it is a condominium than if it is a co-op.

ARE YOU CUT OUT
FOR A FIXER-UPPER?

Buying a fixer-upper can be a good way for anyone on a tight budget to get into a first house. Houses that "need work" can offer tremendous bargains, and you can customize to suit your own preferences. Also, the cost of many of the things you do to enhance the value of a house may be credited against the taxable gain you may make upon its sale.*

The cost of improvements may be deducted from the price appreciation.

Make sure to have a thorough inspection conducted so that you can be certain that all necessary work (at least whatever is necessary to make the place livable) is within your budget. An inspector can determine whether the changes you need (or want) to make are going to affect the house's foundation, or if the place needs total electrical rewiring or a complete plumbing overhaul. This, in fact, is something you want an inspector to check out with *any* potential real estate purchase; even the nicest-looking houses can have major problems.

What you really want to look for in a fixer-upper is a structure of solid integrity that's in need of *cosmetic* surgery—for example, new floor coverings and window treatments, a fresh coat of paint, and some landscaping.

Keep receipts of any and all expenses incurred in upgrading the house, since many of them can help offset your tax liability if and when you sell.

ARE YOU CUT OUT TO BE A LANDLORD?

Another way to enter the real-estate market on a limited income is to buy income-producing property, such as an apartment building or a house with one or more rental units on the property. The rents collected from tenants pay for at least a portion of the mortgage and expenses, which can often make the owner's monthly payments affordable. For the small investor, often an "owner-occupied" piece of income property is most desirable. This provides a home along with the rental income to offset the monthly payments.

The big question, however, is do you want to be a landlord? Do you really want to hear about someone's

---

*When you sell any residence, if you buy another of equal or greater cost within two years, your profits are tax deferred; also, if you are over 55, you may take a one-time tax exclusion from the profit from the sale of your home (see the tax section for more details).

Possible Help for the First-Time Home Buyer

- The Federal Housing Administration (FHA) or Veterans Administration (VA) can get you into a home for very little down payment, if you are eligible, by assisting you in qualifying for a home mortgage. These organizations do not lend the money themselves, but instead *guarantee* the loan—and agree to make good if the borrower defaults. This system of guarantees helps those who might otherwise not be able to secure a mortgage at all. It can lower the down-payment requirements and the rate of interest. Veterans or their surviving spouses may be eligible for VA loans, while the FHA has many loan programs available to a wide variety of people. Contact your local VA or Housing and Urban Development (HUD) offices for further information.

- Any gift or loan from a parent or grandparent can help. It is, in fact, estimated that about one of every three first-time buyers gets some help from a parent or other relative. Sometimes the parent or grandparent is offered, in return, an equity-sharing agreement, meaning that any profit from the sale of the property at a later date would be split. The mortgage-interest deduction can also be shared by the donor as an enticement for giving the gift or loan.

- Leasing with an option to buy can get you into a personal residence and allow you to live there while you save toward the down payment, using your lease payments toward the purchase price.

- Assumable loans can enable first-time buyers to obtain affordable mortgage payments. Some sellers and lenders carry financing that allows a home buyer to assume the current mortgage on a house, which may be at a rate lower than the going rate of interest.

- The seller of the house may agree to help finance your purchase by carrying a mortgage of his or her own. This means that the seller will carry some of the financing and allow you to make monthly payments to him at an agreeable interest rate until the balance has been paid off.

overflowing toilet at 3 A.M.? If not, can you afford to hire a management service (at an average cost of 7–10% of gross rents) to take care of the headaches of apartment management?

Another big question is what's the rent-control

situation in the area? The worst-case scenario is buying in an area without rent control that *becomes* rent controlled while you are an owner. The value of your property could decrease sharply, at least in the short run. If, on the other hand, rent control is already in place, then its restrictions should already be reflected in the selling price of the building; if the rent control were ever repealed, your investment could sharply increase in value.

What about rent control?

CREATIVE FUNDING

Whether it's a single-family house, condo, co-op, fixer-upper, or owner-occupied rental property, the first home has become very difficult for many people in many areas of the country to get into. However, the dream of home ownership is not—and hopefully never will be—completely out of reach.

The dream of home ownership is not out of reach.

We've already discussed the loan provision of a tax-sheltered annuity. Our box shows some other options available to many potential first-time buyers for raising the money for a down payment.

NOBODY EVER SAID IT WAS EASY TO BE A FIRST-TIME BUYER— OR A SECOND-TIME BUYER, OR A THIRD-TIME BUYER

However you decide to purchase your own residence, initially you will probably have to stretch yourself—and your family—financially and, perhaps, emotionally.

This stretching is usually fine, provided you don't stretch too far. There used to be a rule of thumb suggesting that one's housing costs should not exceed 25% of one's income. Today, this rule of thumb must sometimes be stretched to as much as 50% of one's income, depending on other debts and expenses. Ideally, as income increases, what was once 50% can eventually shrink to 25%, and even below.

How much should you stretch?

Most homeowners will tell you that at first they wondered how they were ever going to afford their payments. A few years later, they discovered that their mortgage payments were now the same as the current rent for a one-bedroom apartment in their area.

TSA CAN STAND FOR "TEMPORARY STRETCHING APPARATUS"

Shift from one tax-sheltered investment to another.

Since the interest on your home mortgage is tax deductible, it is possible to temporarily stop funding your TSA in order to get through the first year or two of your home purchase. You won't be increasing your tax burden; in fact, what you'll actually be doing is shifting your dollars from one tax-sheltered investment to another.

If you then get a raise or some form of supplemental income, you can always start making TSA contributions again. It is not unusual for seasoned teachers to enjoy financial growth through both the appreciating value of their home and a tax-sheltered annuity, simultaneously.

ALL HOME MORTGAGES WERE NOT CREATED EQUAL

Home mortgages really do vary from lender to lender. If you think you might want to consider a

---

What to Look for in a Variable-Rate Loan

- How often can interest rates be changed?

- What index is used for these changes?

- Is there a cap? A "cap" is a ceiling that the variable-interest rate cannot exceed. A good annual cap is 1%. A good lifetime cap is 5%—meaning that the most the loan can go up is 5%, and the fastest this can happen is over a five-year period.

- Is the loan negatively amortized? Negative amortization is a kind of interest-rate loophole through which a lender can raise the amount you owe beyond what you originally borrowed. Make sure the variable loan is *not* negatively amortized, if possible.

---

variable-rate loan, there are a number of factors to compare.

On any loan, variable or fixed, find out how many points you have to pay. A "point" is a fee you pay the lender up front. One point is equal to 1% (or .01) of the amount borrowed. If you borrow $100,000, each point is $1,000 cash out of your pocket! (Points may be tax deductible; ask your tax adviser.)

The term of your loan and the frequency of your payments can have a significant impact on how much you pay out in the long run. A 15-year mortgage requires fewer overall dollars than a 30-year plan. A semi-monthly (twice-a-month) payment scheme can also save money. But when you're trying to get into your first home, keeping payments down may be essential.

You can always accelerate your rate of payment whenever you wish. By choosing to pay more, or more frequently, you can reduce the total cost of your loan. Make sure your loan allows extra principal payments—some don't. But it is probably not a good idea to lock yourself into these more demanding payment schemes by signing a 15-year mortgage or agreeing up front to make bimonthly payments. If you do decide to increase or accelerate payments, do it later on, when you can afford to—and with the knowledge that you can always return to the easier payment schedule. Keep in mind that by accelerating the rate or the amount of payment, you reduce the total interest paid, *not* the total principal—and you thus also reduce the amount of your home-mortgage tax deduction. You also need to check to be sure there is no penalty for prepaying the loan.

Give yourself the option of accelerating payments.

DON'T SHOP FOR A HOME UNARMED—MAKE SURE YOU'RE PRE-APPROVED

Most home-mortgage lenders will be more than happy to try to pre-approve you for a loan *before* you ever set foot inside a house for sale. And most home buyers—especially first-time buyers—should be more than happy to get pre-approved. There are several reasons for this:

1. By getting lender approval first, you avoid the pressure and anxiety of hurrying to get a loan in order to back up an offer you've made on a house. With pre-approval you can take your time, picking and choosing until you find the best possible loan.

Pre-approval makes you a more attractive buyer.

2. Pre-approval makes you a more attractive buyer. It may also enable you to get a lower offer accepted, especially by a seller who is anxious to sell or who has had some previous buyers fail to qualify. Being armed with a pre-approval notice guaranteeing you a home-mortgage loan may even enable your offer to be taken over someone else's higher offer that has *not* been pre-approved. There are a lot of real-estate "pseudo-buyers" out there who can make the sale of property a frustrating and costly venture. A sound lower offer is worth more than a higher, but uncertain, offer. (If you are ever in a position to sell, you will probably feel the same way.)

3. Finally, pre-approval can help you focus on what you can really afford so that you won't waste time making an offer on something out of your realistic price range.

Make the lender sell you *the loan.*

To get pre-approved, go to several lenders and present your assets (including your tax-sheltered annuity) and liabilities, along with information about where you plan to buy and how big a loan you estimate you will need. Then sit back and let the lender sell you a loan package.

Keep looking.

If you have trouble getting pre-approved—or approved at all for a loan—keep looking. Sometimes a higher percentage as a down payment (for example, 25% to 30%) can get you over that hump. Also, perhaps you could have a parent or relative cosign the note, thus providing additional guarantees to the lender. Of course, sometimes a lender's refusal to give pre-approval means that a borrower's eyes are bigger than his or her wallet. Being turned down for a loan, painful as it may be, is often a blessing, enabling the home buyer to gain a more realistic perspective—and avoid an eventual catastrophe.

DON'T SHOP FOR A HOME UNACCOMPANIED— USE A REAL-ESTATE BROKER

The services of a real-estate broker can be invaluable to a buyer—and *free* (the seller pays the commission). A good broker can sit down with you, plug your needs into the current market, and outline what you can afford and where you can find it. Use personal recommendations, if you can, to find a broker. Shop around until you're certain that you've found the right person.

BEWARE OF THE INTEREST-RATE CRYSTAL BALL

Most home buyers—especially first-timers—are pretty much at the mercy of current interest rates. They can ill afford to wait for interest rates to fall while real-estate prices are going up. If they shop around, they can often find the best fixed rate possible—yet in two, or five, or ten years, rates might have dropped considerably, leaving them with a 12% or 15% monkey on their back.

Many mortgage holders try to shake this monkey through *refinancing*. They apply for a new loan at a current, lower rate, pay off the old loan in full, and reduce their monthly payments. But refinancing isn't free. You have to pay points (each point, remember, is 1%), and points must be paid up front. Some lenders will allow you to include your points in the mortgage. This means you end up paying a lot of interest on that money. But your upfront costs are much lower. Also, by refinancing you may end up extending your payment schedule beyond its current term.

IF YOU CAN PAY CASH, SHOULD YOU?

Some home buyers are in a position to pay all cash for their purchase—or at least to make a down payment in excess of the usual 20% of purchase price. This is commonly encountered by people who have

---

Refinancing Guidelines:

- Unless you can save a minimum of 2% on your current mortgage interest rate, it's probably not a good idea to refinance (if your current loan is fixed, this is a simple measurement; if your current loan is variable, you also need to consider the cap of your current loan against the cap of any new loan you might be considering).

- Unless you plan to stay in the house for at least another five to seven years, refinancing may likely *cost*, not save, money.

- Do not compare yesterday's fixed rate with today's variable rate (which could, potentially, rise above yesterday's fixed rate).

- Check with an accountant before refinancing a mortgage to determine how much tax-deductible interest you're entitled to. Some of the interest on this new debt may *not* be deductible, and the variables and calculations are too complex for the average consumer to figure alone.

---

recently sold one home and who subsequently buy another for considerably less cost.

From a financial planning point of view, a minimal down payment is usually recommended—even if you can afford more—for the following reasons:

1. Inflation favors using "tomorrow's dollars" rather than "today's"—since today's are worth more.

2. Tax laws subsidize mortgage payments by allowing homeowners to deduct the applicable interest.

3. By making the minimum down payment (usually 20%), the balance of one's funds are available for other diversified investment opportunities.

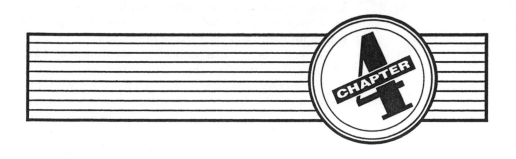

Your Total Financial Picture

While a comfortable—and possibly *early*—retirement may be a priority for many teachers, it is not the only financial goal. There are numerous savings objectives and just as many savings tools.

Prioritize your objectives.

There are four basic financial objectives that you need to prioritize:

1. Growth

2. Income

3. Liquidity

4. Stability

While all four are important, the order of their importance differs from person to person.

If your goals are long-term—children's education, your own business upon retirement—then *growth* would probably top your list of priorities.

If your goals are immediate—enhancing your lifestyle, for example—then *income* may top your list.

If you're uncertain of your goals, then your priority might be *liquidity* (meaning that your investments can be easily converted into cash).

Almost everyone wants *stability* in their investments, but to differing degrees. Some teachers enjoy risk-taking, and the potential financial rewards they may reap.

IF GROWTH IS YOUR PRIORITY

If long-term growth is a priority for you, there are several fairly stable savings tools to choose from. Zero-coupon bonds, real-estate investments, and mutual funds are among the most popular.

Zero-coupon bonds and municipal bonds.

Zero-coupon bonds, which are purchased through a brokerage house or financial adviser, can allow you to enjoy the growth of the bond market for an investment as small as $1,000. Zero-coupon bonds are discounted based on their rate of interest. In other words, rather than having interest paid to you periodically, you can buy the bond for less than its face value, then cash it in when it matures—something like a U.S. Savings Bond, only with a higher yield. Tax-free growth can also be realized with zero-coupon *municipal* bonds.

It is also prudent to look into additional *real estate* as an investment. If you're in a financial position to buy a second home for summers or weekends—even if it's just a log cabin—it could be a very sound investment, one that could give you personal pleasure, financial growth, and tax benefits. The interest on a second home mortgage is fully tax deductible (up to a specified limit high enough for most people not to have to worry about).

Limited partnerships.

You can also invest in real-estate limited partnerships through your financial adviser, for as little as $5,000. Limited partnerships allow many small investors to own shares in very large business ventures. In a *limited partnership,* the general partner(s) are responsible for managing the assets, and they also generally assume any liability beyond the limited partners' investment. Many limited partnerships do not make income distributions to the limited partners until the assets are sold (anywhere from 3 to 15 years down the line), and thus are long-term investments.

In addition to real estate, limited partnerships are formed to finance cable-TV systems, oil and gas ventures, and even such exotic—and speculative—areas as motion pictures, popular music albums, and musical comedies. Real-estate limited partnerships include apartment houses, shopping malls, mini-malls, office buildings, and parking structures. Obviously, you cannot spend a quiet weekend inside "your" mini-mall—it probably won't even get you a discount from the mall's dry cleaner—but if the project is in the right place at the right time and turns a solid profit, you could be in for a good return on your money (taxable upon sale).

Since the passage of tax-reform legislation, limited-partnership investments—once intended as tax write-offs—now emphasize growth (though there is, of course, no guarantee). Before investing any of your hard-earned dollars in a limited partnership, find out about the track record of the general partners: how long they've been managing this type of investment, and what kind of returns they have generated for their limited partners in past projects.

Mutual funds that invest in high-quality blue-chip stocks also provide the opportunity for long-term growth. These funds are comprised of hundreds of different securities, giving you maximum diversification for your dollars. Look for a solid ten-year track record with reasonable fees and charges. Make sure the particular mutual fund gives you the flexibility to shift your money between the vendor's various funds (stock fund, bond fund, money-market fund) so that, if you so desire, you can benefit from trends in our economy. Be sure that such transfers can be done easily and inexpensively.

Look at the ten-year performance record.

Variable annuities and *variable life insurance* contracts offer the opportunity to tax-defer earnings on a select group of investment options provided for under each plan. These programs are most suitable for accumulating retirement capital, since government restrictions on withdrawal and the possibility of adverse short-term market conditions often preclude earlier access to funds.

Fixed Annuities. In addition to the fixed tax-sheltered annuity (TSA) discussed on page 31, life insurance companies offer fixed annuities which consumers may purchase with *after-tax* dollars, either in a lump sum, or with periodic purchase payments. When selecting this conservative investment for your portfolio, make sure to compare features such as interest rate guarantees, withdrawal flexibility, and, of course, insurance company ratings and safety. The main benefit of these annuities is the accumulation of interest on a tax-deferred basis. Because of this feature, the government normally does not permit withdrawals to begin prior to age 59½ and assesses a 10% penalty for any such premature distribution.

SAVING TOWARD YOUR CHILDREN'S EDUCATION

Perhaps the most common reason that teachers want stable long-term growth for their savings is so they can save for their children's college educations. Teachers with children tend to put college tuition among their top savings priorities. As a close friend and teacher once said: "I'd like to think my daughter will earn a full academic scholarship to MIT, but I wouldn't want to entrust her future purely to the grading whims of my colleagues."

Pay for college in advance.

Some institutions of higher learning will now let you prepay tuition at current tuition prices, under the fairly sound assumption that the cost of a college education is going to continue to increase at a high rate. In some cases you can even get your money back if your child decides not to go to that college.

Teachers who have accumulated enough in a tax-sheltered annuity can use the TSA's five-year loan provision to pay part of a child's college-education expenses. Another popular way to create a college nest egg at a very low tax rate is to save money in the child's name so that the earnings are taxed at the child's bracket—which, assuming the child doesn't do commercials or have a paper-delivering empire, is at a low rate. Until recently, you could do this regardless of the child's age. The law, however, has been changed so that the savings accounts of children under 14 are now automatically taxed at the parents' bracket. With that in mind, you may need to begin saving at a tax-free lower interest rate, shifting the money to a taxable higher-yield investment upon your child's fourteenth birthday—assuming that the law has not changed again by that time.

IF INVESTMENT INCOME IS YOUR PRIORITY

Those teachers who either need or want current income produced by their investments have numerous choices. Mutual funds can offer income, as well as possible tax savings through various types of bond investments, including tax-free municipal bonds. They are also fairly liquid. Other stable income-producing investments include treasury bills (T-bills), government bonds, certificates of deposit (CDs), and money-market funds.

Treasury bills are issued by the United States Treasury, mostly in order to finance the growing national debt. *Government bonds* are issued by the federal government and by state governments to help finance diverse government projects. *Certificates of deposit*, issued by banks and savings and loan associations, offer you relatively high interest in exchange for having your money tied up for a specified amount of time. For a competitive rate of interest without the time lockup, money-market funds are a better choice.

Bills, bonds, and CDs.

The yields on the above investments may not be astronomical, but neither is the risk.

If, on the other hand, you have the time, talent, and temperament for the roller coaster of higher-risk investments, you may want to investigate using a

Higher-risk investments.

portion of your capital to trade in stocks and bonds. But in general, you'll want to avoid such exotic investments as arbitrage (trading foreign currencies), gold mines, Third World bonds, subordinated debentures (a type of bond), penny stocks (stocks issued by start-up corporations with no track record), junk bonds (high-yield/high-risk bonds rated less than "investment grade"), real estate time-shares, commodities (buying and selling shares of tradable commodities, such as cattle, soybeans, and frozen orange juice), and commodity futures (in which you try to predict the price of a given commodity at some future time).

YOUR MONEY IS WORTH ONLY WHAT IT WILL BUY

Precious metals. Some teachers, ever conscious of the potential of inflation in the economy, will invest some of their savings in gold mutual funds. These fluctuate in relation to the price of gold and to the stock market (both inflation sensitive). These gold (and other precious-metal) funds should not be confused with high-risk mining investments, which are, most often, a hit-or-miss proposition. Gold-stock mutual funds may invest in companies that do some mining operations, but they are diversified enough to somewhat offset the risk. Other inflation-conscious teachers have been known to buy gold coins or bullion as an inflation hedge. Such precious-metal investments are economically sound, but they can be risky because they may be lost, stolen, or destroyed—and the cost of a safe-deposit box must be factored into the investment equation. In general, keep no more than 5–10% of risk capital in this category of assets.

IF IT SOUNDS TOO GOOD TO BE TRUE, IT ALMOST ALWAYS IS

We have all heard horror stories about "sure-fire," high-yield investments that have collapsed. Rare-coin deals, trust-deed pools (in which investment dollars are pooled together and used to finance trust deeds, but with each investor having no recourse in the event of a default), oil drilling, precious-metal mining—many of these are unregulated even by state governments, and some can be outright con jobs. They'll offer high rates of return, pay interest for a short time, and then go out of business, pocketing everyone's principal. Such schemes capitalize, in part, on the delusion that it is possible to get rich quickly and easily.

It isn't.

Investors—especially small investors—are better served trying to get rich slowly. Promoters are usually the only ones who get rich quickly.

Always read the fine print, *and* the bold print (sometimes deception is staring you right in the face). There are, for example, triple-A-rated bonds issued by major corporations at amazingly attractive interest rates—and denominated, they will tell you in small letters, in a foreign currency. This makes the highly rated bond subject to the whims of currency fluctuations. And be *extremely* skeptical of any investment sold exclusively—and in a high-pressured manner—over the telephone. A knowledgeable and trustworthy financial adviser can help you to steer clear of anything that sounds too good to be true.

Precious metals.

INVESTING IN YOURSELF

On the more personal side, some teachers prefer to save toward an entrepreneurial dream, such as opening their own private school. This, like a home, is an investment that may pay more than financial rewards alone. But no matter how much you trust and believe in yourself, such a venture is a high-risk—uninsured—undertaking.

The savings made *toward* that initial investment in a business, however, should be made conservatively. In other words, you don't want to lose the money before you've reached the point of starting the business.

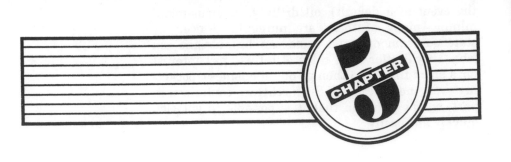

A Smart Investment– Paying Off Those Credit Cards

Debt is nothing to be proud of.

Some people believe that the true measure of wealth is not how much you *own*, but how much you *owe*. This couldn't be further from the truth.

Debt is nothing to be proud of. It's nothing to be mortally ashamed of, either, since it is so widespread (and since our own government has a severe debt problem). But it is, most certainly, something to be grappled with before it is too late.

When debt begins to spiral, you can find yourself paying interest on the interest, and never making a dent in the original debt. You could spend the rest of your life paying for that VCR or dishwasher.

AN EQUITY LINE OF CREDIT MAY BE YOUR ANSWER

Some people take an equity line of credit against their home or other property to pay off credit-card debt. If you can get a 10–12% loan on which the interest may be at least partially tax deductible, and pay off debt increasing at a rate as high as 18% (non–tax deductible), you can at least cut your losses. By taking an equity line of credit, you can also consolidate the debt from two, five, or even ten different credit cards into one (sobering) lump sum—and then slice up those cards so you never use them again.

Cut your losses.

Many lenders offer equity lines of credit. To determine whether you qualify, and for how much, these lenders will look at the appreciation of your property since you bought it, any home improvements you've made that may increase its value, and how much of your mortgage has been paid off. Bear in mind that if it is a variable equity line of credit, the interest rate could go up along with the prime rate. Most equity credit lines now have a cap (five points is a good cap to look for and to discuss with your accountant, who can verify the loan's tax deductibility).

IF YOU DON'T OWN PROPERTY

If you are buried beneath credit-card debt and cannot get an equity line of credit, the most reasonable solution may be to make certain temporary sacrifices in order to make larger payments on the debt, while making no additional credit-card purchases. There are now public agencies and other organizations that give budgeting and other advice to people with severe debt problems. Debtors Anonymous uses the Twelve Steps of the Alcoholics Anonymous program to help its members abstain from spending money they do not have. They have local offices in most parts of the country, and they can provide you with a questionnaire to help you determine whether you suffer from chronic compulsive spending.

You can get help.

BANKRUPTCY IS *NOT* THE FREE RIDE IT'S CRACKED UP TO BE

Some people believe they can erase their debts and start over by filing for bankruptcy. But there is no "fresh start" after the often humiliating process known as "Chapter 7," "Chapter 11," or "Chapter 13." Having defaulted on one's past debts makes it extremely difficult to get credit in the future (and those companies that will extend credit often require large amounts of collateral and charge exorbitant interest rates). Because bankruptcy can be a complex area, you may wish to retain an attorney to advise you on which, if any, of the three types of bankruptcies is appropriate for your particular situation.

ALTERNATIVES TO CREDIT CARDS

A lot of people use the equity line of credit, rather than credit cards, to finance major purchases. Those who have accumulated enough in a tax-sheltered annuity may use the five-year TSA loan.

For convenience in making smaller purchases, it may be wise to maintain one or two credit-card accounts, using self-control and paying off the debt each month to avoid both late charges and inflated interest.

Control your credit cards or get a debit card.

If you lack self-control with credit cards (and you are certainly not alone if you do), then you may have no choice but to cut up the cards. However, you may still be able to maintain the convenience of a credit card with a *debit* card. Some banks will issue you a piece of plastic that looks like a credit card but functions like a check. This card can be used in all of the same kinds of transactions as a credit card. Charges are deducted directly from your checking account, so you need to keep careful records so that you won't run the risk of bouncing a check—but you certainly won't run the risk of compiling significant credit-card debt.

A Smart Investment—Paying Off Those Credit Cards

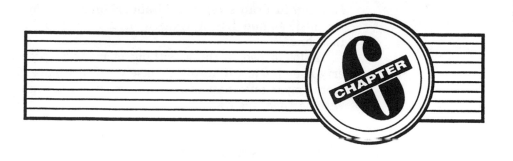

CHAPTER 6

Protecting What You've Worked So Hard to Accumulate

Most people think of insurance as a necessary evil—but the key word is *necessary.* If you own a home or have any savings or other assets, it is essential that you protect them so that no matter what happens, your life savings and retirement planning will not be wiped out.

The key word is necessary.

Your insurance needs can be grouped into two categories: property and personal.

Property refers to what you own. Your property-insurance needs include auto insurance, homeowner's or renter's insurance, and other liability coverage.

Personal insurance refers to disability insurance, major medical and hospitalization insurance, and life insurance.

A lot of people think nothing of insuring property, then neglect to insure themselves. Since you are more important than what you own, we will begin with personal insurance.

THE CAFETERIA OF HEALTH-CARE BENEFIT PLANS

Most school districts provide their employees with health-care benefits. Often, there is a choice, usually between a traditional health-insurance carrier and a health-maintenance organization (HMO). Deciding which plan to go with can be difficult, especially for those who already have a family physician with whom they are comfortable.

HMOs: The One-Stop Approach to Medicine

The major types of HMOs.

An HMO is an organization that delivers broad, comprehensive health-care services to a specific group of voluntary subscribers for a fixed periodic prepayment—rather than on a fee-for-service basis. There are two broad categories of HMOs: (1) the group practice prepayment plan (GPP); (2) the individual practice association plan (IPA).

The GPP plan is a kind of all-purpose medical clinic. Subscribers get access to a wide variety of medical, and sometimes dental, services, and their families' medical needs can usually all be met at one or more specific locations. Sometimes there is a choice of doctors within the HMO, and sometimes not.

The IPA plan involves foundations or groups of physicians who remain in private practice as individuals or small medical groups while offering their services to HMO subscribers who pay a fixed periodic prepayment. This arrangement ensures a choice of doctors.

HMOs may sometimes cost more than traditional health-insurance plans, but these costs are often more than compensated for by lower deductibles and more extensive coverage for prescription drugs, extended nursing care, and other important services. Also, because HMOs benefit financially when their subscribers do *not* get sick, they may place greater emphasis on preventive medicine. Some HMOs offer free periodic physicals as part of this commitment.

Traditional Health Insurance

Those who have a family physician not associated with an HMO may prefer a group health-insurance policy that allows them to keep their current doctor. While traditional health insurance generally means smaller payroll deductions, deductibles may be higher. Also, most of these insurance carriers have schedules of what they consider "reasonable and customary" charges. If a doctor's fees exceed those schedules—and they often do—the subscriber is responsible for the difference. "Preferred provider" organizations (PPOs) have, in recent years, mitigated such discrepancies. The PPO concept is the traditional health-insurance carrier's answer to the HMO. The insurance company makes advance agreements with specific physicians and hospitals—about fees and other charges—and then approves those health-care vendors for their subscribers.

"Reasonable and customary" charges.

Many insurance companies now publish a list of those doctors, hospitals, and other medical services whose prices have been pre-set and agreed upon. Often, this provides a greater selection than an HMO. Also, you may still use physicians not on the list, but it will probably cost you a lot more.

YOU'RE WORTH A MILLION

Ultimately, your health-care decision should be about good health and longevity more than about dollars and cents. Good health is a priceless asset, well worth almost any affordable price.

Do you need to supplement your coverage?

Teachers' health-care benefits, of whatever type, are often quite comprehensive. Sometimes, however, they might not satisfy your needs, and you may need to look into some kind of supplementation.

The whole point of insurance is to keep you out of a county hospital or a bankruptcy court. Find out what the cap is on all your employee insurance benefits. If the benefits stop much before $1 million on major medical and hospitalization, you may want to seriously consider some kind of supplemental policy. If your spouse works and also receives employee benefits, his or her plan can usually be coordinated with yours to provide as much as 100% coverage.

YOU'RE ALSO WORTH THIRTY OR FORTY THOUSAND PER YEAR

Many school districts provide group disability insurance, which pays you in the event that an injury or illness prevents you from working for an extended period of time. If your district does not provide disability coverage—or if the coverage falls considerably short of your current earnings—it is a good idea to buy a private disability policy to ensure that lost earnings would not throw you into financial peril.

Protect yourself against protracted illness.

In order to keep premiums low on such a policy, you may want to consider a three- or six-month waiting period rather than the usual 30 days. (The waiting period is the period of time between the date you incur a covered disability and the date benefits become payable.) Most people who are unable to work for a short time manage to get by; it is only protracted disabilities that threaten one's long-term financial stability. By choosing a longer waiting period, you could save enough in premiums to help get you through that waiting period if you were ever seriously disabled.

INSURE YOUR RETIREMENT IN CASE OF ILLNESS

Guarantee your medical benefits.

An important part of retirement planning is to make sure that you will have sufficient health-insurance protection, especially major medical and hospitalization. Eligibility for Medicare, the federally funded health-care system for persons over 65, may coincide with your planned retirement. If it does not, find out how much medical insurance is going to cost you during the gap. If it will be extraordinarily expensive, or if you discover that you are potentially uninsurable (due to a past illness or a preexisting medical condition), you should probably see about converting your teacher group-policy benefits. This can sometimes be done on a guaranteed basis (meaning that the company has to insure you).

Find out the time frame, cost, and coverage of this conversion, and compare it with any alternatives you might have. Conversions can be quite expensive and fairly limiting. But you should have *something*— at least until Medicare kicks in.

Even when you do become eligible for Medicare, you will probably have little or no protection for long-term nursing-home stays or custodial care at home. Supplemental long-term care plans can offer this needed protection. (Long-term care policies may be purchased separately from a basic Medicare supplement plan.)

You aren't likely to get this kind of top-quality policy if you're already sick. The time to look for

---

Look hard—you should be able to find a long-term health-care policy that gives you the following features:

- Waiting period of no more than 20 days before benefits begin
- Maximum benefit period of no less than four years
- Full benefits for skilled nursing care
- Full benefits for intermediate care
- Full benefits for custodial care
- Daily nursing-home benefit of no less than $80
- Home health-care benefits, regardless of whether there has been prior hospitalization or nursing-home confinement
- Coverage for Alzheimer's disease
- Policy guaranteed renewable for life
- A or A+ rated carrier

---

long-term health care is *before* retirement, and certainly before the onset of any major illness.

Regardless of the circumstances of your policy (that is, full or supplemental coverage), make sure, if possible, to get a policy that is guaranteed to be renewable. This way, if you do ever suffer a protracted illness, the insurer cannot individually cancel your policy and leave you uninsured and without protection.

With disability insurance, you can sometimes get not only guaranteed renewable protection, but protection at a guaranteed premium rate as well.

You will, of course, not find a long-term guaranteed rate on any *medical* insurance policy. In the coming years, the cost of health insurance—like that of medical care—is certain to increase. We are all going to have to help foot the bill, unless the government does something radical. Until such time, taking high deductibles can help keep your health-insurance costs to a minimum. It bears repeating: taking good care of your health is the wisest investment you can make.

A TRIO OF LIFE INSURANCE OPTIONS

If you have anyone financially dependent on you, you'll want to consider owning your own life insurance plan in addition to any coverage provided by your employer. Three important items to look at when you consider a life insurance policy are viability of the insurance company, amount of coverage, and type of policy.

Be sure to consider the stability of the insurance company.

Choosing the right carrier for you is often a matter of getting the most coverage for your money while enjoying the security of knowing the company will be around—and solvent—when the time comes for your beneficiaries to collect. Refer to the bottom of page 35 for information about independent services which rate the solvency of life insurance companies.

Deciding how much coverage to buy can involve calculating the present and future financial needs of your beneficiaries against your current assets. These needs may include paying off a cumbersome home mortgage, child care, a college education fund, funeral and other final expenses, and generation of a dependable income to maintain an appropriate lifestyle. A popular shortcut—also a method for those with very little savings or other assets—is to simply multiply 5 to 7 times your current annual income (a $30,000 income would indicate the need for life insurance coverage of between $150,000 and $210,000).

The three most commonly sold life insurance policies today are traditional whole life, term life, and universal life. Each plan has benefits and drawbacks. Compare all three types of coverage to decide which type is best suited for your life insurance needs.

Traditional Whole Life

This type of policy is purchased, in full, over a designated period of time—anywhere from 1 to 30 or more years. It can even be purchased all at once, in one lump sum. The cost of the policy is based upon the age of the insured and other actuarial health factors. Premiums are level, much like a home mortgage, so that there is normally no fluctuation. Whole life policies cost relatively more early on, but less in the long run. Also, whole life policies build equity—known as "cash value"—which you may borrow against or which is paid out to you if and when you surrender your policy.

Whole life builds cash value.

Term Life Insurance

If whole life is like the home mortgage of life insurance, term life is the rental or leasing agreement. This type of policy gives coverage for as long as you pay the premiums, but pays out no cash value. If you stop paying the premiums after 5 or 10 or 20 years, the insurance company owes you nothing—and this is a serious concern since the premiums become prohibitively expensive as you get older. Term life is an excellent vehicle for a young man or woman without much disposable income, who wants to insure his or her spouse and children until the better long-term life insurance plans are within financial reach. (Term life plans can usually be converted to whole life plans without evidence of insurability.)

Term life is more affordable.

Universal Life Insurance

This type of policy falls somewhere between whole life and term. It offers lower term-like premiums but also builds cash value. Interest rates credited on these policies by each insurance company determine future premium costs, coverage amounts, and how much cash value you build up. While it is quite flexible, universal life offers virtually none of the premium and benefit guarantees that whole life or term life often contain.

"Fixed" (as opposed to "variable") life insurance policies may be covered under a state guaranty fund. Refer to Chapter 2 for details. (This protection may apply to both the death benefit and the accumulated cash value of the policy.)

INSURING YOUR ASSETS WITHOUT HOCKING THEM

Take large deductibles.

The most sound approach to the ever-increasing cost of property insurance can be summed up in three words: take large deductibles.

Property insurance should be for emergencies only, not for small mishaps that can be handled out-of-pocket. This is true with auto insurance, homeowners' insurance, and virtually any other kind of property insurance. Taking a high deductible can greatly reduce both your insurance premiums and the chance that making a claim will increase your rates. Of course, you must then be prepared to pay for minor mishaps (i.e., up to $1,000 or $1,500). But if you were to raise your deductible to its maximum and then have good luck (with no accidents, fires, or damage to your property) for three or four years, you might save enough in premiums to more than compensate for any future out-of-pocket expenses.

When you make a claim—even a small one—the insurance company not only has to pay your claim, but it also incurs numerous other expenses, from estimating to processing. When you take the maximum deductible and thereby create potential savings for the insurance company, the company can then pass at least some of its savings on to you.

Insurance is a gamble. The company that writes you a policy is gambling on you—they hope your life will be problem free. Why not have the same confidence in yourself by taking a high deductible on your property insurance? Take guaranteed savings on premiums for your auto, home, and other property insurance, rather than speculative risks that will save you money only *if* you are careless or unlucky.

Insurance is a gamble.

DO YOU NEED AN UMBRELLA?

If you own a home, you probably need at least $1 million in liability coverage to protect your home and your other assets. An umbrella policy can help to ensure this protection.

An umbrella policy maximizes personal-liability coverage. It can simultaneously increase your existing liability coverage on your home and car. Even if you don't own a home, measure your net worth and see what you might have to lose in a liability lawsuit—and then protect yourself.

Protect yourself from a liability lawsuit.

JUMPING SHIP CAN BE COSTLY IN THE LONG RUN

One potentially *un*wise approach to dealing with the increasing cost of any insurance is to change carriers every time your rates go up. There is no guarantee that your new carrier won't raise your rates even more in a year or two.

Also, if you have to furnish evidence of insurability after you have changed carriers, you may discover that you may not be as insurable as you were when you signed up with the original carrier. You may rate as a higher risk and may be turned down or given restrictions. In changing health-insurance policies, for example, you could be excluded from benefits for such things as pregnancy and maternity care or psychiatric treatment.

The best way to determine your needs is to consult a qualified expert, someone who can show you all the available policies and explain the advantages and

Consult an expert. disadvantages of each. In choosing an insurance broker, use the same guidelines as you would in choosing any financial adviser. Try to get a referral from someone whose finances seem to be in sound order. Find out how long the broker has been in business and where she or he was trained. Find out, too, whether the broker works for only one insurance carrier. If this is the case, find another broker. You need an independent broker, someone who will make objective comparisons among all of the major carriers for you so that you'll get the most for your money.

If you can find someone who can handle all your needs—that is, for both insurance and investments—this can simplify things and help in the integration of your financial planning. However, a financial adviser who tries to wear too many hats may wind up not wearing any of them very well.

Probably the ideal situation is to have two advisers (one for investments and personal insurance, the other for property insurance) who know each other and can work together, when necessary, for your benefit. An easy way to achieve this is to start out with one adviser whom you like and trust, and then have her or him refer you to others with different specialties.

Insurance You Can Do Without:

- Credit life and disability plans (on major purchases.)
- Accident-only policies.
- Rental car insurance, if your rental is covered by your personal automobile policy.
- Flight insurance.
- Cancer insurance.
- Uninsured Motorist coverage on your automobile policy. (Ask your agent to explain what it actually is!)

Protecting What You've Worked So Hard to Accumulate

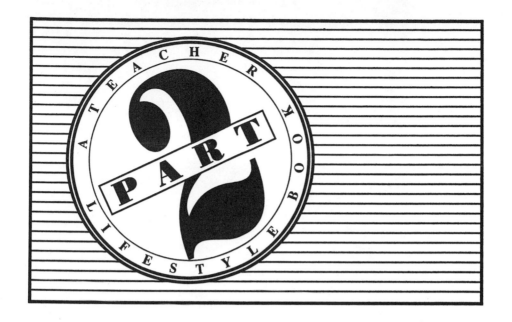

PART 2

A TEACHER LIFESTYLE BOOK

Increasing the Pie: Tips for Supplementing Your Income

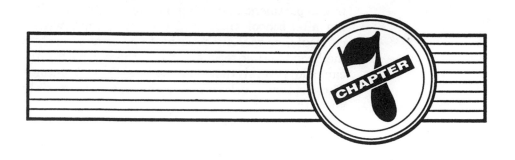

Moonlighting–Making Extra Money During the School Year

Despite the arduousness of their profession, many teachers somehow find time for extracurricular employment. Not only can such jobs supplement income, help toward the realization of financial goals, and provide tax benefits, but they can also—especially in the case of self-employment—bring personal satisfaction and enjoyment.

ONE SKILL ALL TEACHERS HAVE: TEACHING

Nobody has to tell you about the extra income opportunities available at school. These include extra-duty *Teachers are in demand.*

pay, department managing, mentor programs, advising after-school clubs and activity groups, writing curricula, or making presentations of new teaching methods to other teachers. All of these opportunities can add several thousand dollars to one's income. These options work well for some teachers, especially since the work is mostly done right at school, often during school hours. One drawback, however, is that many of these opportunities are not permanent. This is all the more reason to examine some alternative ways to supplement income. If your at-school income ends, you'll already have some ideas about how to replace that extra cash upon which you've come to depend.

Teach English as a second language.

Teachers who live in cities with substantial numbers of recent immigrants can make excellent money teaching English as a Second Language (ESL). ESL classes are taught through community colleges, adult-education programs, language schools, and private citizenship courses; contact these programs directly to inquire about part-time employment. An ability to speak a foreign language helps, but it is *not* usually a prerequisite. ESL classes focus on basic and practical applications of the English language, such as ordering food in a restaurant, asking for help at a hardware store, or answering questions at a job interview. Students tend to be very attentive and responsive, not needing much external motivation—and there are usually no papers to correct!

People with an ability to communicate effectively and to teach with both enthusiasm and patience are almost always in demand—not just for ESL classes, but for any and all adult education. Other types of classes usually meet one or two nights a week, and the subjects taught can range from basic skills—such as mathematics or American government for adults seeking their high-school diplomas—to such diverse areas as creative writing, driver's education,* and computer programming, operating, or repair. (Adult education, by the way, may also be a place to *find*

---

*Most states require special certification in order to teach driver's education.

and learn a skill that might produce supplemental income.)

TEACHERS HAVE A WAY WITH KIDS

After spending all day with children or adolescents, some teachers cannot wait to get as far away from them as possible. Others, however, look forward to being with kids in a more relaxed atmosphere, such as an after-school group that provides activities—and sometimes tutoring—to kids who need after-school care. Such groups, which are something like quasi-day camps, are always looking for counselors who have experience with kids.

Teachers can even start their own after-school activities groups (a riskier, but potentially more lucrative, approach). The initial investment in this kind of enterprise—which can often be shared by two or three entrepreneurial teachers—must be enough to cover advertising and liability insurance. *Your own teaching business.*

Advertising need not be expensive. Fliers placed in and around schools, and possibly a mailing to local parents, might be all that's needed to fill your desired rosters.

In this litigious world, liability insurance is a *must,* and it is probably the most prohibitive cost of this kind of business.* Many states now regulate after-school activities groups and require liability insurance, certification of the group's director, special driver's licenses, first-aid certification, and maximum adult-to-child ratios. You may or may not need to furnish transportation, depending on the size of your community. But assuming you live in a fairly large city and hope to attract kids from more than one school, you will almost certainly need to use your own car(s) and possibly even purchase a used van. You may not need an actual piece of property. Depending on state regulations, some after-school groups can meet in parks and other public facilities.

---

*The cost of such liability coverage may vary considerably, depending on where you live.

Working with Kids on a Smaller Scale

Tutoring—an intimate learning situation.

Needless to say, an enterprise such as that just discussed is consuming of time and energy. It is, most certainly, not for everyone. What is *ideal* work for any teacher who would like to work with kids after school—and make good money—is private tutoring.

Many teachers find this type of work to be not only lucrative but also intrinsically rewarding. Tutoring gives a teacher a chance to work in the most intimate learning situation—one on one. If the tutoring is done at the student's home, insights into the lives of the average student can be gained, insights that can be useful back in the classroom.

Other teachers have cashed in on the ever-growing need for entertainment at children's birthday parties. They've discovered that parents are willing to pay top dollar for an hour or two of singing, game playing, puppet shows, some rudimentary magic, and a good costume and makeup.

TEACHERS WORK WELL WITH PEOPLE

As noted, the teaching profession requires not only good communication skills, but also patience—with parents as well as with students. These skills are in great demand and suit many teachers for the huge and ever-growing service sector of our economy. No, we're not talking about flipping burgers after school. The service sector includes a wide range of jobs that can be both personally and financially rewarding.

Real estate is a potentially lucrative part-time job.

Real estate is one potentially lucrative people-intensive industry employing part-timers, including teachers. Some real-estate companies will train teachers or pay their way through real-estate school, with evening or weekend classes provided. A great deal of the work can be done after school hours, since most sellers and buyers have 9-to-5 jobs.

The travel industry can also offer opportunities for teachers. Some travel agencies will train you to be a part-time sales representative and get you certified and on the national list of travel agents, even if all you do is book tickets and coordinate trips for friends and relatives. This can take no more than a few hours a week—with some of that time spent at home, some at the travel-agency office. The money may not be outstanding, but the travel perks and other benefits can make it worth the while. Some travel-agent discounts can save as much as half the cost of traveling. Also, you are eligible to make a number of "familiarity trips" (also known as FAM trips) in order to familiarize yourself with the hotels, tours, and any other services you might have to recommend to customers in the future. Much of the expense of this kind of trip can be tax deductible, creating additional savings.

The travel industry can provide income and discounts.

Teachers can also make extra money as tour guides. Tours use some of the skills you would use for field trips, only with adults instead of (or as well as) children! Such a job not only supplies extra income but can also help you to develop a job skill that could, at some future date, help you to get a job in a foreign country.

VIRTUALLY ANYTHING REQUIRING A LICENSE OR CERTIFICATION IS A POTENTIAL OPPORTUNITY FOR A TEACHER

No, we're not talking about practicing medicine or law (although there are some legal services you can be certified to perform). Teachers can become certified as appraisers for real estate, antiques, rare coins, or vintage cars. In fact, any personal interest you may have that translates into a state or local license may also translate into extra income. Again, the best idea for you may likely spring up simply from your own interests.

A TEACHER'S SPECIFIC SKILLS CAN TRANSLATE INTO EXTRA MONEY

A math teacher—or any other teacher with an aptitude for mathematical calculations—can supplement his or her income doing tax preparations for three-and-a-half months each year. Some tax-preparation services offer courses that run about 13 weeks. These are difficult courses, requiring a lot of study, but they qualify—and certify—students to do tax preparations for any service in need of help during the crunch from January 1 to April 15. The work can be done on evenings and weekends, and most tax-preparation services have liability insurance that covers its pre-parers for errors and omissions. One of the most delightful benefits of this seasonal moonlighting is that you'll probably be able to prepare your own taxes (though you'll have to be careful which friends and relatives you tell about this newly acquired talent!).

English teachers, who may or may not correct papers on a regular basis, may have a talent for proofreading. Free-lance proofreaders are needed by publishers of books, magazines, newspapers, manuals, and other printed matter. Some publishers also hire free-lancers to do copy editing, which involves reading a completed manuscript and correcting spelling, grammar, syntax, and factual inaccuracies. Obviously, such opportunities are much greater in major cities—especially New York—but teachers can also find opportunities through university and many other presses throughout the country.

Teachers Have Skills Outside Their Realm of Teaching

Teachers who possess a sound knowledge of computers can combine that expertise with the ability to teach in order to reap a good deal of extra income. They may not need to look any further than their own school or school district to get paid as a consultant, coordinator, and hands-on trainer. Small businesses also need help in setting up and operating their computer systems. Many first-time computer buyers will pay good money for help in getting acquainted with their new systems once they've discovered that they can't just plug the computer in, turn it on, and go right to work!

Teachers can also turn their own computers into machines of commerce. Those with sufficient software can cash in on word processing. Many small businesses—as well as college students and writers—supply a never-ending need for fast, clean typewritten pages.

Put your computer to work.

Those teachers with more sophisticated computers and access to a compatible laser-jet printer can use desktop publishing to produce professional-quality newsletters. Potential clients include small businesses, nonprofit organizations, and even some small corporations, as well as certain individuals (such as seminar speakers). Teachers can even make extra money using their computers and printers as typesetting machines for the school newspaper.

Even if you don't have access to the latest state-of-the-art desktop-publishing equipment (which constitutes a hefty investment), you can still produce résumés, events calendars, and other promotional materials to enhance your income—in some cases without having to devote very much time to the tasks.

Beyond Computers: Some Other Valued Skills

Athletically inclined teachers, whether or not they teach physical education during the day, can moonlight by teaching aerobics classes or giving private athletic-training sessions. They can, in this way, maintain their own personal exercise regimens and make extra money in the process.

Other teachers may choose to moonlight by teaching karate, grooming dogs, or providing party entertainment. One junior-high science teacher moonlights as a traveling disc jockey, spinning his records at weddings, parties, and Bar and Bas Mitzvahs—and, once, at the grand opening of a discount shoe store!

TEACHERS CAN MAKE HOBBIES PAY FOR THEMSELVES— AND FOR A LOT OF OTHER THINGS

Turning a hobby into a business means that you'll probably enjoy the work, and that you'll have flexibility. If family or other demands increase, or if you just grow a little weary, you can always take a break or try something new.

Hobbies are a business you're sure to enjoy.

A biology teacher, for example, turned his love of the ocean into a large source of income by turning his boat into a business. During the school year he leases the boat for parties and fishing expeditions on weekends and holidays. That income alone more than covers the boat payments and maintenance. Then, when summer comes, he alternates between making money and having fun with his boat. At the end of the year he enjoys a tax savings, as well.

Other hobbies that can be turned into part-time businesses include flower arranging, carpentry, and homemade crafting. Handmade creations can be sold at flea markets, retail stores, and home boutiques.

Home Business Adventures

Just as you can now purchase almost anything you can imagine by mail order, you can also *sell* a wide variety of products—from ginseng to kitchen utensils—out of your own home. If you have an empty garage or another part of your home to store an inventory of merchandise, along with advertising and postal supplies, you can turn some of your free time into both extra money and tax deductions.

The initial investment can be as little as a few hundred dollars.

The initial investment can be as little as a few hundred dollars, depending on the minimum order of your product supplier. Advertising can begin in the classifieds.

Teachers can also supplement their incomes with multilevel marketing. There are a number of companies that will make you a part-time, free-lance sales representative or distributor of their products. Some of these companies require an initial investment, which must be weighed against a realistic projection of how much you can sell in the first year or two (earnings are strictly on a commission basis). It is also important to make sure that you believe strongly in the quality of the products, since it can be frustrating to try to generate enthusiasm about a product that you do not respect. Some teachers are able to find products they believe in and can do very well selling and distributing them. Regardless of how much money they earn, they all enjoy tax advantages, such as being able to write off a part of their home as an office and deducting travel and other expenses incurred in trying to make sales.

Some teachers have capitalized on the home-boutique boom of recent years by turning their homes into virtual retail stores once, twice, or even three times a year—and pocketing as much as $10,000 in additional income.

Capitalize on the home-boutique boom.

The best times to hold a home boutique include the late November/early December Christmas shopping season, and the spring (for graduation, Mother's Day, and Father's Day). The host usually charges a yearly membership fee to all craft sellers—to help cover the cost of advertising, cleaning, and refreshments—plus a 10–15% commission on all sales.

A home boutique is a large undertaking, involving a lot of hard work and some financial investment, but it can be quite rewarding. For some, the best part is being able to sell their own wares commission-free (though it's also possible to make a sizable profit without selling a single piece of one's own merchandise).

Be Alert: An Idea for a Side Business Can Strike at Any Time

An elementary school science teacher used to moonlight during the school year, and sometimes work summers, editing and transferring videotapes for a small company that produced presentational videos. This company also did what are known as "air checks." For example, if an attorney was going to be on the news and wanted a professional-quality copy of his two-minute segment, the "air checkers" would record and edit the segment for a fee.

What our friend noticed, after a while, was that most of the air checks were being done for local advertising agencies and advertisers (car dealers, carpet stores, and so on). These companies wanted to monitor whether their commercials were being played when stations claimed to be playing them. With that in mind, the teacher/editor started his own cottage industry. He bought several black-and-white television sets and hired people to act as monitors.

The monitors watched TV all day and kept track of commercials. Then he hired out his company to the very same advertisers who had been ordering the air checks from the editing company.

If you can think of an unsatisfied need, either in business or on a personal level, you may have an idea for a small, home-based, part-time business that can supplement your income and give you tax benefits.

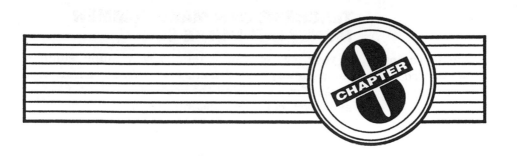

Teachers with Summer Jobs

Teachers who do not wish to teach summer school can find other ways to keep the money flowing (or at least to create tax breaks) during the summer. Even if you teach in a year-round school, you may often have four to six week breaks in which to earn extra money.

IF YOU ALREADY MOONLIGHT DURING THE SCHOOL YEAR

Most teachers who already have an extra source of income throughout the school year will work at their extra source full-time during the summer. This, of course, is easiest when your extra work is self-employment and when it involves a service. The biology teacher with the boat (mentioned in the previous chapter) is a case in point. Any business that involves entertaining or supervising children is a natural for summertime expansion.

TEACHERS CAN MAKE SUMMER MONEY OUT IN THE SUN

Summer camps always need counselors.

If your love of kids extends beyond June, summer camps always need counselors. There are a wide range of camps to suit the needs of a variety of kids—and they can also potentially suit the needs of teachers looking to make summer money.

If you'd rather not take care of children all summer, there are other ways to have fun and make money. Many resorts hire extra summer help, and so do ball parks. A social studies teacher who used to teach in a Milwaukee suburb spent his summers selling peanuts, hot dogs, and soft drinks at Brewer games during the summer. He'd hustle for the first seven innings, making enough commissions for the day, and then, if it was an exciting game, he'd take it easy and watch the last two innings.

A music teacher works summers ushering at the Hollywood Bowl, the outdoor venue of the Los Angeles Philharmonic. It doesn't pay very much, but she gets to hear the concerts for free.

A surprising number of teachers make extra summer money laying bricks, hammering nails, and hauling any number of construction materials on large and small projects. The money, they say, is decent. The work is physically draining, but it doesn't involve much mental stress—a nice change from the classroom!

National parks and theme parks offer interesting jobs.

Depending on where you live, there may also be summer work available in local and national parks and at theme parks (one teacher spent a summer portraying Goofy at Disneyland!).

WORKING ABROAD

If you like to travel and want to make money, it's possible to do both. You can, at the very least, break even by teaching English in a foreign country. A number of teachers have financed summer vacations and turned a profit by teaching in Europe and Asia. Because of the value of the yen, at the moment Japan is probably the most lucrative market for teachers of the English language.

Like ESL students in the United States, the students abroad tend to be highly motivated and courteous. And you don't have to be an English teacher, since the curriculum focuses mainly on basic communication skills. Such work can also enable you to meet interesting people wherever you're visiting, and to learn some of the native language of that country.

You don't have to be an English teacher to teach ESL.

For those of you with a particular interest in working abroad, consult the companion book to this series, *Travel Tips for Teachers*, by Sunni Bloyd. It provides full coverage of the many travel and work opportunities available to teachers.

TEACHERS CAN ALSO MAKE SUMMER BUCKS WITHOUT THE ADVENTURE

Married teachers can sometimes find interesting summer work through a spouse's business or place of employment. The pay may not always be great, but there can be opportunities to become eligible for Social Security or certain employee-benefit programs. And sometimes just being able to spend the extra time with one's spouse makes the job worthwhile.

Other summer opportunities may grow out of a teacher's sphere of expertise and interest. One high-school art teacher spends his summers drawing storyboards and performing other artistic tasks in the animation process for Walt Disney Productions.

Remember, whatever your particular skills, they are probably in demand somewhere in the business world. Just don't be *too* successful out there in the mainstream job market, or the teaching profession may lose you for good!

Whatever your skills and interests, they're in demand somewhere.

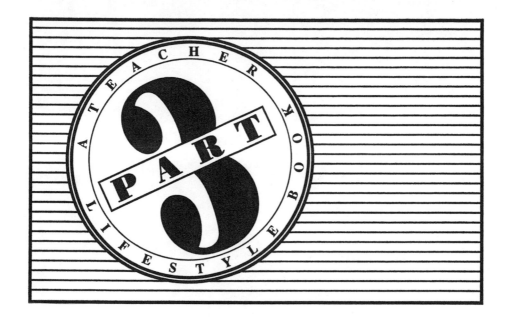

PART 3
A TEACHER LIFESTYLE BOOK

Taxes
and
Legal
Concerns

A LITTLE KNOWLEDGE
CAN SAVE A LOT OF MONEY

Whether you have a personal accountant, use a tax-preparation service, or prepare your own income-tax returns, you can always benefit from a knowledge of some of the nuts and bolts of the tax codes and what they probably mean to most teachers. Tax preparation, as you will see, does not begin when you hand over your W-2s and a shoebox of receipts to an accountant or tax-preparation service. Tax planning is a continuing challenge. It begins at the beginning of each calendar year and continues until that year's returns have been filed.

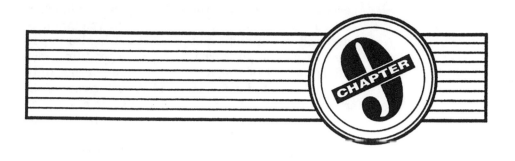

Do You Need an Accountant or an Attorney?

If you enjoy preparing your tax returns, then you may be well served to do it yourself. You need to have a feel for what is reasonable so that you can be legally aggressive enough to get the deductions you are entitled to without triggering an audit each year. You also need to have current knowledge of changes in the tax code—and you need the capacity to understand IRS tax explanations. Much of the tax-code rules are extremely convoluted, making for tedious reading (and rereading) of IRS booklets. (There are now toll-free IRS hot lines throughout much of the country, but the U.S. General Accounting Office recently discovered that about one-fourth of all the information dispensed over these hot lines is *incorrect!*)

If you do elect to prepare your own tax returns, and you own property, make sure you are fully aware of all the laws regarding home-mortgage interest deductions, depreciation and amortization, and prop-

Many teachers can benefit from professional help.

erty taxes. Otherwise, you might be making inadvertent donations to the U.S. Treasury—or you might be destined for an audit and penalties. It is also important, if you do your own taxes, to begin filing soon after the first of the year rather than waiting until the last weekend before April 15. And be aware of the rules for extensions. For example, you are allowed an extension of four months without penalty, but you must file a form in order to get it. If you owe money, an estimated amount that's within 90% of your actual tax must be paid by April 15, or you will be charged interest and penalties.

Most teachers who own property or have other investments that create complex tax calculations use professionals to prepare their taxes. Others who can probably benefit from professional help in preparing their tax returns are those with self-employment income, tax shelters (such as limited partnerships), or foreign-earned income.

Some teachers use tax-preparation services or private tax preparers for reasons of time and convenience, and because of their belief that the tax savings created by a professional can more than pay for the fee (which can be tax deductible).

THE THREE BASIC VARIETIES OF TAX ASSISTANCE

Accelerate your refund.

If you have one source of income, bank interest only, do not own property, and do not itemize deductions, you can probably get adequate tax assistance from a tax-preparation service. There are now a number of businesses offering computerized tax calculation, with direct computer transmission to the IRS. This process is supposed to speed things up (by up to three weeks) for those expecting refunds.

If you own property, you may be better off with a public accountant (PA); they have more training and can also help fight the IRS if your return is challenged.

If you own your own home, have more than one source of income, and have investments and/or tax shelters, the services of a certified public accountant (CPA) would probably be helpful.

Do You Need an Accountant?

As with any other professional advice or service, the most reliable way to find competent help is usually through the recommendation of a friend or colleague who seems to have his or her affairs in sound shape. If you already use a financial planner, stockbroker, or insurance broker, and you are happy with that person's credentials and performance, you may want to get a recommendation from him or her. An accountant may also be an "enrolled agent," which entitles him or her to represent you in tax matters before the IRS. Only a CPA, Enrolled Agent, or an attorney may act in this capacity on your behalf.

If you are new in town, use professional organizations (such as your local CPA society or the National Association of Enrolled Agents in Rockville, MD) for referrals. They will usually give you three names and phone numbers, which should be sufficient to make a selection.

How much should you pay?

In selecting tax assistance, first find out about fees. Fees generally range from $50–$250 per hour, depending on the complexity of the taxes and on whether this is a one-time service or an ongoing professional relationship. (A CPA who advises you on taxes and other financial decisions year-round is going to charge considerably more than someone who prepares tax forms once a year.) Fees also vary depending on where you live. Common sense and information on what friends and relatives with similar tax needs pay for services should help you determine what you will need to pay.

If a tax professional's fees do not seem reasonable to you, you need not ask him or her any further questions. If the fees are within reason, find out how long the person has been in business (five years or more is a good criterion). If you are going to be paying for an ongoing professional relationship, ask about the person's availability during times of the year other than the tax season. Also, ask for names of clients you can call as references.

WHAT ABOUT LEGAL ADVICE?

If your financial situation is very complex, you may wish to enlist the assistance of a tax attorney or other specialized legal adviser. Some areas that often require sound legal advice include the following:

- Preparation of a will.
- Setting up proper guardianship.
- Deciding on and executing a living trust or other type of trust arrangement.
- Probating an estate.
- Bankruptcy (See Chapter 5).
- Preparation of a "living will."
- Divorce settlements.
- Business start-ups or dissolutions.
- Holding title to property.
- Gift-giving and estate planning.

To locate a legal specialist in your area, contact the Attorney Referral Service of your city, county, or state bar association.

Tax Tips Every Teacher Should Know

R egardless of who does your taxes, there are some things that you and every other educator can benefit from knowing.* If you do your own taxes, this information is a *must*. If you use a professional, you can still maximize the time and tal-

Keep those receipts!

---

*The wide diversity of state and local income tax laws makes it impossible to give the details of these. We will, therefore, deal almost exclusively with federal income tax, though many of these principles may also apply to the rules of many state and local tax codes.

It should also be noted that tax laws are open to interpretation. For specific tax information applicable to your individual situation, please refer to IRS or state tax publications or to your independent, qualified tax counsel. All figures in this chapter are for use in helping to calculate taxes only for calendar year 1991.

ents of your tax preparer (and sometimes save money in fees as well as in taxes) by being forearmed with a little knowledge—and a lot of receipts. Tax preparers appreciate knowledgeable clients who plan ahead, keep clear records, and have a good idea of where they stand in relation to the tax codes.

THE NUTS AND BOLTS OF INCOME TAX

The amount you owe in federal income tax is primarily a function of two things: your net taxable income, and your tax bracket.

Reduce your taxable income.

Your *net taxable income* is defined as how much income you have had in a given year minus everything the government allows you to subtract, including standard deductions or itemized deductions. When you (or a professional tax preparer) set out to reduce your tax obligation, you do it by reducing the net taxable income. This is one of the reasons why tax preparation begins at the *beginning* of the calendar year. Once the year is over, the only thing you can do to reduce taxable income—with rare exceptions—is to claim the deductions you've created during the tax year. Think of it this way: the IRS is going to take a piece of your pie. With the right tax planning, you can trim your pie down considerably before they take that bite.

There are a number of ways to legally reduce taxable income. We will deal specifically with those most applicable to teachers. First, however, it is important to clarify what the IRS considers to be income.

THE MANY FACES OF INCOME

Common sources of taxable income for teachers include the following:

- Teaching salary
- Salary from a second job
- Business, self-employment, or free-lance profit

- Interest (from a bank,* teachers' credit union, or other source) that does not qualify for tax-free status; also, any interest over $1,000 in the name of dependent children under the age of 14, if you wish to include it in your tax return.

- Dividend income from stocks or other investments[†]

- Refunds of state and local taxes

- Alimony received (not including child support)

- Capital gains on the profit from stock sales, bond sales, real estate, and other assets (real estate gains can be tax-deferred if the money is put into a like investment within a specified amount of time).

The IRS also includes such things as contest winnings, game-show winnings, and gambling winnings as sources of income. In cases where such sources are applicable, the assistance of a CPA is a good idea come tax time.

THE UNTOUCHABLES: INCOME THAT IS NONTAXABLE

Some sources of a teacher's income are nontaxable. These include:

- Foreign-earned income, up to an IRS-specified amount[‡]

- Dependent children's wages, up to an IRS-specified amount

- Tax-free or tax-deferred interest (such as that generated from an IRA, TSA, or tax-free municipal bond)

- Tax-free dividends

- Gifts of cash or property

---

*Banks are required to send an account to the government of how much taxable interest they have paid you each tax year on form 1099.
†Like banks, regulated investment companies are required to send a record of your account to the government.
‡Check into restrictions regarding a return to the United States during any period of overseas employment.

The Untouchables: Income That Is Nontaxable

- Federal income-tax refunds, if you elected the standard deduction in the previous year

- Nontaxable state and local income-tax refunds, if you elected the standard deduction in the previous year

Fellowships and grants.

- Fellowships or scholarship grants, when used to cover tuition, fees, books, and course equipment (grants for room and board and other living expenses are considered taxable income)*

- Prizes and awards for literary, educational, scientific, civic, or charitable achievements where recipient was not *obliged* to perform such work

- Reimbursements for board-approved educational courses

- Reimbursements for interviewing fees

- Reimbursement for moving expenses, if paid by the school district and if expenses do not exceed the cost of moving

- Profit on the sale of a personal residence under certain conditions: (a) if profit is put toward the purchase of a new home of equal or greater cost within two years;† and (b) if the profit is $125,000 or less,‡ you have owned and lived in the home for three of the last five years, and either you or your spouse is at least 55§

- Rent received from a boarder for less than 15 days

- Wage continuation or disability income paid during sickness or disability through a policy in which you paid the premiums

- Worker's compensation or other accident-insurance benefits

Health-insurance payments.

- Health-insurance payments made by an insurance plan in which you paid the premiums, even if payments exceed your related medical costs

---

*Fellowship and scholarship monies granted prior to August 16, 1986, are fully tax exempt.
†This deduction may be taken as many times as a taxpayer meets the requirements.
‡This amount may increase or decrease in years to come.
§This deduction may be taken only once.

- Damages paid to you for personal injury sustained in an accident

- Damages paid to you for breach of contract, slander, or libel (subject to certain restrictions)

- Repayment of the principal of any loans you make (the interest *is* taxable)

- Inheritances (inheritance tax is *not* income tax)

- Death benefits paid by employer (up to $5,000;* anything beyond this amount is taxable income for the beneficiary)

- Child-support payments made in accordance with a divorce settlement

- Alimony payments received on an informal basis (i.e., not court ordered), and not claimed as an alimony expense on former spouse's income tax return

TRIMMING THE PIE

Even with all of these sources of tax-free income, most teachers are still going to find that nearly all of their income is taxable. There are, however, a number of ways in which the IRS allows you to decrease the taxable amount of that income.

First, the Freebie

By following the instructions on a tax return, it is pretty hard *not* to get your personal exemptions by simply filling in the appropriate box and then entering the appropriate amount in the appropriate box (though it is possible to be entitled to additional dependent exemptions of which you are not aware). Currently, each exemption—personal as well as for dependents—enables you to deduct $2,150 from your gross income.†

---

*This amount may increase or decrease in years to come.

†The exact amount of this deduction changes almost yearly, usually fluctuating upward—to the benefit of taxpayers.

Dependents Come in Many Shapes and Sizes

In simple terms, a dependent is anyone who is financially dependent on you for most of his or her living expenses. The IRS allows you to claim the following as dependents:

- A child living with you if he or she is a full-time student, up to age 24

- A child not living with you but receiving more than 50% of his or her support from you (children of divorced parents may be claimed as an exemption by only *one* parent per tax year)

- Any relative of any age (child, stepchild, grandchild, sibling, stepbrother, stepsister, half-brother, half-sister, parent, stepparent, grandparent, nephew, niece, uncle, aunt, or in-law) who receives more than 50% of his or her support from you. It is possible, however, to get a dependent exemption for someone for whom you contribute as little as 10% support. If this friend or relative is supported by others who do *not* claim him or her on a tax return, you can—with the approval of the others giving this person support (and with form 2120)—claim the person as a dependent. It is even possible for those sharing in the support of a dependent to agree to take turns, from year to year, claiming him or her as a dependent.

- Anyone living with you for the whole year and receiving more than 50% of his or her support from you, subject to their income level

Trimming the Pie a Little at a Time

Another way to reduce taxable income is through itemized deductions.* These are various expenses

---

*If you do not have enough itemized deductions to make itemizing worthwhile, you may still take the standard deduction. As of this writing, these deductions are as follows:

Single	$3,400
Married	$5,700
Head of Household	$5,000

that the IRS allows you to deduct from your gross income. There are hundreds of allowable deductions, many with specific rules. We will examine some of those most useful to teachers.

Educational Expenses*

Expenses used by a teacher as part of continuing education are allowable deductions. Such expenses can include tuition payments for course work, college textbooks, registration fees, student-body cards, necessary laboratory materials, tutors, college parking stickers, transcript and degree costs, and student health insurance. Any expenses incurred in the preparation of term papers or graduate theses—such as the costs of research, typing, duplicating, or mailing—are deductible.

Continuing education expenses are deductible.

The above expenses are deductible whether the goal of one's education is to earn higher salary within the same area of teaching or to enter a new area of teaching.

Other Job-Improvement Expenses

Any other expenses you incur in the pursuit of a higher salary and/or a better teaching job are deductible. These expenses include employment-agency fees paid in connection with a change of jobs within the educational field—even if you do not get another job as a result.

Many of the Things the Teaching Profession or School District Requires You to Pay for

Virtually all teachers pay union dues, and many pay membership fees to professional organizations related to the teaching profession, as well as teaching-credential renewal fees. Some teachers are still re-

Union dues and membership fees are usually allowable.

---

*Educational expenses are deductible to the extent that they exceed 2% of your adjusted gross income; for example, if your adjusted gross income is $20,000, the first $400 of educational expenses are not deductible.

quired to have tuberculosis X-rays taken. In some school districts teachers are required, under certain circumstances, to help with the costs of hiring substitute teachers. And in some districts teachers must make indemnity payments—for example, posting bond for sabbatical leave. All such expenses are usually allowable deductions, but may be subject to the 2% rule cited earlier.

Teaching Expenses

Most teachers find themselves using at least some of their own money in order to purchase items necessary for performing an adequate job. Such expenses are generally regarded as deductible by the IRS. They include:

- Office furnishings and supplies (both at school and at home) needed for planning curricula, grading papers, or performing any other part of your teaching responsibilities (note, however, that the actual space in your home is *not* deductible under these circumstances).

- Any telephone calls you make from your home to administrators, parents, or other teachers as part of your teaching responsibilities.

Special clothing or equipment.

- Any uniform or other type of special clothing purchased solely to meet a particular teaching-job requirement (such as woodshop coveralls or a choir leader's gown).

- Equipment necessary to your job—such as tape recorders, attaché cases, and calculators—that you yourself have paid for. Such items must be used *only* in connection with teaching. You may also be able to deduct larger, depreciable items, such as typewriters and photocopy machines (along with any expenses relating to their maintenance, service, cleaning, and repairs), as long as these machines are for the sole purpose of helping you in the performance of your teaching duties.

- The cost of hiring readers or other assistants to help you in your professional duties.

- Materials you purchase to enhance learning in the classroom. Expenses can include art and science materials, books, videotape and film rentals, sheet music, audiotapes and records, shop tools, maps, athletic equipment, and projection equipment.

Expenses Incurred in Becoming a Better Teacher

We've already mentioned deductions for formal education as a tool toward enhancing teaching skills. However, "enhancement" deductions do not *have* to be related to formal education. Any expense incurred in maintaining or improving your teaching skills is allowed to be used as a deduction. Such expenses can include magazine and newspaper subscriptions, books, maps, scholarly journals, tickets to lectures regarding your particular area of teaching, and even films, concerts, plays, museum memberships and admissions, or sporting events. The only requirement for tax deductibility is that these expenses relate directly to the subject you teach and that your reason for purchasing these resources or attending these events is to make you a better teacher.

Trips, lectures, journals.

Much of the cost of a sabbatical, if incurred in the pursuit of improving teaching skills and knowledge, can be deducted. Such expenses can include leave-of-absence expenses and travel and research expenses.

Any other teaching-related trips you make during vacations for the purpose of improving your teaching skills can be deducted, as can any local travel expenses to and from any class, seminar, or other event you are claiming as a teaching expense.

Etc., Etc. . . .

There are a number of other allowable tax deductions that, while not being of use *primarily* to teachers, are nevertheless of use to many educators—especially those earning employee wages from a second job at some time during the tax year. These other deductions include:

- Home-mortgage interest

- Gifts and entertainment that are necessary in the pursuit of a better job, or that are expected of you in a current job

- Medical expenses, including prescription medicines and drugs, to the extent that they exceed 7.5% of your adjusted gross income. (For example, if your adjusted gross income is $20,000, the first $1,500 of medical expenses are not deductible.)

- Expenses you incur in connection with charitable work for any organization granted tax-exempt status by the IRS, including travel miles or actual travel expenses incurred.

- Training expenses in connection with a second job

- Purchased materials or other expenses required by a second job that are not reimbursed (other than transportation to the place of employment)

Casualty and theft losses.

- Casualty or theft losses to the extent that they exceed 10% of your adjusted gross income (the first $100 is also not deductible). For example, if your adjusted gross income is $20,000, loss due to theft would have to be more than $2,100 in order for you to claim any deduction.

- Alimony payments made in accordance with a divorce settlement

ITEMIZATION DOES NOT ALWAYS ADD UP

Some teachers do not accumulate many deductible expenses every tax year. However, they are still eligible for the standard deduction. This deduction—a result of the recent tax reform law—gives anyone who does *not* itemize deductions an automatic deduction from his or her adjusted gross income. If, in a given tax year, you add up all of your itemized deductions and the sum is less than the standard deduction for your filing status, you will want to elect the standard deduction (this is an important consideration when it comes to planning your tax year, which we will examine shortly). The standard deduction, it should also be noted, does *not* exclude any self-employment deductions (see note on p. 100).

TRIMMING THE SELF-EMPLOYMENT PIE

Teachers who do extra free-lance work or who run their own small or home businesses can enjoy a broad range of income-tax deductions that are completely separate from itemized deductions.

Self-employment is treated by the IRS as a business venture. Only the *profit* (which is calculated on a Schedule C form) is taxable. Any reasonable expenses incurred in the pursuit of self-employment income can be deducted from that income.

Only profit *is taxable.*

Self-Employment Can Produce a Negative Pie

If your Schedule C deductions exceed your gross self-employment income (that is, if you spent more on this self-employment than you made), you can claim a *loss*. This loss is deducted from your adjusted gross income.

For example: A teacher's adjusted gross income is $20,000 after all other deductions. This teacher ran a desktop publishing company out of his home. Because it was his first year, his expenses were high ($5,000) and his clientele was small (income was $3,000). He can claim a $2,000 loss and reduce his adjusted gross income to $18,000, saving several hundred dollars in taxes.

Some teachers can benefit from claiming a loss by turning a hobby into a business. This is perfectly legal, as long as the purpose of the business is to make money. The IRS does not stipulate that you cannot *enjoy* self-employment or sole proprietorship if it isn't making money. There are no legal limits to the size of the loss, provided that you can substantiate it. Nor is there any legal limit to how many years you can claim a loss. If your business goes for three to five years without a profit, the IRS may become suspicious and demand an audit. But, again, if you can substantiate all of your expenses and prove that you are in business to make money, you will not have

Take advantage of more than 200 deductions.

violated the tax laws. So there is no reason not to take advantage of the more than 200 deductions allowed on a Schedule C.

Self-Employment Means Making Social Security Contributions

Anyone with a self-employment profit over $400 is required to pay Social Security tax of 15.30%, but only 92.35% of this figure is charged, if you're below the current maximum wage base of $53,400.* What this means is that if after subtracting deductions you wind up with a $2,000 profit from self-employment or sole proprietorship, you are required to pay a little more than $283 in Social Security taxes. This is all the more reason to get the maximum allowable deductions by knowing what they are and by planning each tax year accordingly.

Self-Employment Also Means Schedule C Deductions

The actual number of allowable deductions on a Schedule C—"Profit or Loss from Business (Sole Proprietorship)"—form is too high to list them all here. Following are a few examples:

Advertising Expenses

Business cards, accountants, gas, stationery—can you deduct?

Any money spent on fliers, posters, mailings, classified ads, newspaper or magazine advertisements, coupon offers or premium giveaways, promotional prizes, donations or contributions to any organization that provides advertising in exchange, business cards, or any other means of advertising a service, product, product line, or resale business can be fully deducted from gross self-employment income.

Accounting and Auditing Expenses

Any money you have to spend to keep books or inventory or to prepare tax returns for self-employment is deductible.

---

*This percentage has, for the past few years, been on the rise, and it could increase in years to come.

Automobile Expenses

To the extent that a particular car or vehicle is used in the earning of self-employment income, you can depreciate the cost of that car. This is done by following an IRS formula based on the cost of the car and the year in which it was purchased, or 27 ½¢ per business mile driven may be used as an alternative. The end result is that over a five-year period, beginning with the first year you own the car, you deduct a portion of its cost—based on how much the car is used for this business. So, for example, a $10,000 car, used half for pleasure and half for a self-employed business venture, might allow you a $1,000 per year deduction (one-fifth of the purchase price per year is $2,000; half of that—because the car is half used for the business—is $1,000).

You can also deduct the cost of gasoline, oil, and other maintenance (including tune-ups, washing, and waxing); garage rent; insurance (as well as the cost of any damage *not* covered by insurance); repairs; registration; and other fees. It is common for a self-employed teacher to claim 50% of his or her car expenses on a Schedule C, meaning that half of the miles on the car were in direct connection with self-employment, while the rest of the car's use was for commuting to his or her teaching job (*not tax deductible*) or for recreation (*also not tax deductible*). The IRS may require a mileage log in order to confirm the extent to which a vehicle was used for self-employment. The IRS will allow you to simply deduct a predetermined amount per mile rather than calculate the automobile expense.

Other Transportation Costs

The cost of transportation by taxi, bus, train, and even airplane, provided that the sole purpose of such travel has to do with your self-employed business, is deductible.

Office Expenses

Such expenses can include office supplies, stationery, and telephone and other utilities, as well as painting, decorating, cleaning, and maintenance. You can also deduct office rent or depreciate the cost of office

Take off a percentage of your mortgage or rent.

property. If, like a great number of self-employed teachers, your self-employed office is somewhere in your home, you may deduct that part of your home (as a percentage of the total cost of your mortgage or rent and utilities) if that office is used primarily for your self-employment. Say, for example, that you live in a three-bedroom house, and one of the bedrooms serves as your office. If this room accounts for one-fifth of the total square footage of your house, you may deduct one-fifth of your mortgage or rent.

You may *not*, however, deduct any part of your home if your Schedule C shows a *net loss* after all deductions. This raises an interesting question: what if taking a home-office deduction means that you end up with a net loss, when without that deduction you would show a net profit? In such a case, you can elect to exclude certain other allowable deductions so that you may use the home-office deduction, provided that it still leaves you with some amount—however small—of net profit. (A percentage of mortgage interest and property taxes may still be deductible, without regard to the "net loss" situation.)

Professional Fees
These include fees paid to lawyers, brokers, agents, or any other experts whose services you retain in direct connection with your self-employment.

Theft and Other Losses
Losses from a home office, or that are otherwise connected with self-employment, can be deducted. Losses may be due to theft, fire or other natural disasters, or bad debts. Unlike itemized casualty-loss deductions, losses on Schedule C need *not* exceed 10% of gross income plus $100.

Gifts
Gifts to customers may be deducted up to a value of $25 per recipient per year. You may also deduct gifts you give to others with whom you do business in your self-employment. For example, a teacher who also does free-lance writing may deduct the cost of gifts for an agent, editor, researcher, or anyone else whose cordial relationship is potentially profitable in this self-employment.

Home Entertainment

If it is for the above reason, entertainment may also be fully deductible. If, for example, a teacher/antique appraiser hosts a dinner party for antique dealers who might provide work for him, he may deduct the cost of food, drinks, service, and any other expenses necessary for a successful dinner party. This deduction is limited to 80% of the actual cost.

Research or Education

When it is undertaken in order to acquire or sharpen a skill or perform a task in direct connection with self-employment, the cost of research or education is deductible on a Schedule C. For example, a teacher who writes plays may deduct the cost of theater tickets, theatrical literature and periodicals, classes, or reading fees. Teachers who have their own mail-order businesses may deduct the cost of mail-order seminars, wholesale-product catalogs, and any travel expenses incurred in order to attend product conventions.

Taxes Other Than Federal Income Tax

Such taxes are deductible if they relate directly to your self-employment. Potentially deductible taxes may include city or state gross-receipts taxes, state unemployment-insurance tax, state income tax, state unincorporated business tax, real-estate tax, tangible property tax, customs, import or tariff tax, license tax, and nearly any other business tax.

Retirement-Plan Contributions

A portion of your self-employment income can be placed into a Keogh or Simplified Employee Pension (SEP) plan that defers taxability of your self-employment income and earnings.*

Schedule C's Can Come in Pairs— or Threes or Fours

Teachers can earn extra income from more than one self-employment source. In such cases, they are required to file a Schedule C for each venture. During

You may have more than one outside business.

---

*If your self-employed business has any employees, however, they may also have to be included in these plans.

Trimming the Self-Employment Pie

the school year, for example, a teacher might do private tutoring, against which he or she can deduct such expenses as travel to students' houses, Christmas and birthday gifts for students, workbooks, and other materials. Then, in the summer, he or she might work as a free-lance landscaping consultant, deducting the costs of tools, materials, travel expenses, and advertising, among other things, on a separate Schedule C for this business.

DON'T LEAVE WITHHOLDING TO THE WHIMS OF YOUR PAYROLL DEPARTMENT

As a salaried teacher, you are given a choice of how many withholding allowances to declare on your paycheck. The number of allowances will determine how much federal income tax (and state income tax, where applicable) is taken out of each check. It is important to try and project what your total tax liability will be by the end of the year so that you can select the correct number of withholding allowances at the beginning of the year. If not, you could face one of two problems:

Withholding too much—or too little.

- *If you withhold too much*, you could be giving the U.S. Treasury an interest-free loan for more than a year. Yes, you will eventually get the money back in the form of an income-tax refund—but in the meantime that money *could be* earning interest for you.

- *If you withhold too little*, you run the risk of violating the tax laws and possibly having to pay a penalty in addition to the tax you owe. The law states that you must withhold an amount within 90% of your actual tax liability. The only way to do that is to project the year's adjusted gross income (salary, interest, dividends, Schedule C income, and all other taxable income, minus deductions) and make the necessary withholding allowances on your W-4 and on your state tax forms.

Employers *will not* tell you if you are over-withholding or under-withholding; they will merely withhold whatever your W-4 and their withholding tables tell them to.

Projecting Your Tax Liability for the Coming Year

A good way to begin is with last year's tax liability, since it is likely to be similar to that of the coming year. Account for any increase in salary and any fluctuations in your allowable deductions. If you have other sources of taxable income, include these in your projections. Also consider any potential change in filing status (upcoming marriage, divorce, or children to be born). Once you have projected your tax liability, you can easily figure out how many withholding allowances to claim.

The payroll department of your school district should have up-to-date withholding tables.* Once you have approximated your projected tax liability, ask to see these tables. Working backward, determine how many allowances to withhold for the coming year. If your income changes drastically during the course of the year, you can always alter the number of allowances accordingly.

You can change the amount of withholding during the year.

PROJECT YOUR SELF-EMPLOYMENT INCOME

If your annual income from self-employment or from a home business exceeds a certain amount, the IRS requires you to file, and pay, quarterly estimates toward your annual income and self-employment tax obligations. Since these estimates must be filed four times, you can use not only last year but also last quarter as a guide.

IRA AND TSA WITHDRAWALS: KNOW YOUR OPTIONS

When you become eligible to start receiving disbursements from an IRA or a tax-sheltered annuity, you also become responsible for paying tax on the

---

*Some districts use individualized tables, different from those provided by the IRS.

money you receive. You may elect to have the insurance company, or other provider, withhold income tax, in much the same way that the school district does for your salary. Or, you can make quarterly estimates yourself with or without the help of a tax professional. Predetermined withholding is probably more convenient, while quarterly estimates may give you more cash in hand.

ANOTHER REASON TO ESTIMATE THE COMING YEAR'S INCOME: PLANNING DEDUCTIONS

Planning is the key.

Knowing your approximate tax liability can help you in planning certain deductions. For example, if you project a small tax liability, you may want to postpone certain allowable deductions that you might not have available every year, such as educational travel. The time to make such plans is at the beginning of the tax year, or at least *during* the tax year—not when it's over.

If you know in advance that a particular expense is tax deductible, you can usually better use the tax advantage. Travel is a good example. If you plan to deduct the expenses of a trip as something that will enhance your teaching skills, certain preparations can help. It is usually advantageous to determine, before you even make travel arrangements, not only where you are going and what you are going to do, but what is going to make the trip an educational tax deduction. This way, you can plan your itinerary accordingly—and use that itinerary as part of your evidence if you are ever audited.

Careful planning will not only protect you in case you are ever audited, but it can also help *prevent* an audit—as can some other safeguards.

TIPS TO HELP YOU AVOID AN AUDIT

Prevent an audit.

Most audits begin with a random sampling. The IRS, unable to check everyone, will shuffle its computerized files and pull out a small number of names—somewhere between 1 and 2% of taxpayers. Those returns are carefully examined for anything suspicious. If everything on a particular tax return adds up and nothing extraordinary is found, it is unlikely that the audit will proceed any further. But if the examination *does* turn up some peculiarities, an IRS auditor may soon be on his way.

A good accountant or tax preparer should be able to help you avoid errors and omissions. An experienced tax professional may also be able to tell you whether some of your deductions, though legitimate, are extraordinarily high and may therefore arouse IRS suspicions. Of course, if the deductions are legitimate, you are under no legal obligation to change

---

Factors Likely to Trigger an Audit

In addition to illegible returns, unsigned returns, incorrect Social Security numbers, and inaccurate mathematical calculations, the following items are likely to trigger IRS suspicions:

- *Unreported income.* The IRS has records not only of all W-2 salary wages, but also of all 1099 self-employed income statements, interest, and other miscellaneous income. Failure to report any such income will arouse the attention of the IRS.

- *Omitting other important information.* Such information may include the Social Security numbers of dependent children over one year of age.

- *Claiming deductions that no longer exist.* Even in cases where the law has just been changed, tax returns with outdated claims for such deductions as state and local sales taxes, 100% consumer-interest charges, or working-couple deductions may instigate an audit. The IRS logic is that if you are out of touch with current tax codes, you could easily have committed other inadvertent errors.

- *Claiming deductions that have never existed.* Examples may include personal legal expenses for divorce, adoption, wills, and trusts; personal auto registrations; utility taxes; garbage-collection fees; or real-estate closing expenses.

- *Formal membership in barter clubs.* Barter clubs are organizations in which members trade goods and services with one another without declaring these transactions, thus avoiding paying any tax. For example, a dentist will do bridgework for a plumber who will, in turn, replace a garbage disposal for the dentist. The IRS, needless to say, is likely to take a hard look at such activities.

Tips to Help You Avoid an Audit   *113*

them—but you may wish to do so to help avoid future inconvenience, depending on how much of a tax savings is at stake.

Hope for the Best, Prepare for the Worst!

Keep accurate and thorough records of all expenses you plan to deduct, including receipts, travel logs, and other supportive materials.

If you deduct part of your automobile expenses on a Schedule C form, it is a good idea to keep a daily account of the self-employment business miles driven, and their purpose. This will enable you, if audited, to support the automobile-expense deductions. If you attend an educational seminar and plan to deduct the expenses, pick up program schedules, pamphlets, and other related materials, and make notes or recordings to go along with all travel, hotel, and meal receipts. Any and all supportive receipts should have your notations on them as to the exact expense from which they resulted.

Keep organized as you go along.

If you lose an important receipt, canceled checks and credit-card statements can take their place. If, for some reason, you are without *any* support of an expense deduction, do not panic. You may still be able to, in good faith, use the deduction if it is within certain reasonable limits. There is, for example, a recently reported case of a teacher claiming $125 for miscellaneous educational materials; the teacher had no records to back up this deduction, yet a tax court still allowed it. An experienced accountant with clients in the field of education should usually know what the IRS considers "reasonable" for a particular kind of deduction at a given time.

Finally, and perhaps most importantly, if you ever have to deal with an IRS audit, keep a positive and gracious attitude. It is not the job of an IRS auditor to get you in trouble. Rather, it is this person's job to make sure you've paid your fair share of taxes. If you have, there's nothing to worry about. A little kindness toward the auditor may not cancel an error you or your tax preparer might have made—but it can't hurt, either.

Financial Planning Is Not Deprivation

THE FUTURE LOOKS BRIGHT— SAVE AND SPEND WITH CONFIDENCE

It really is possible for a teacher to enjoy a reasonably high standard of living and also save for the future. Teachers enjoy the security of knowing their skills will always be in demand (within the educational system and elsewhere), and this kind of security is helpful in planning for—and succeeding at—long-term financial growth.

Teachers who have outlined their financial goals and have begun to save toward them often find that they enjoy what money they do spend more, even if it is less than the disposable income they had before financial planning. In other words, once financial goals are in place and the necessary savings are being made, pleasure spending can be guilt free!

Pleasure spending can be guilt-free!

115

SPEND TO ENJOY—YOU DESERVE IT

Money is valuable to the extent that it enhances the quality of life. For some teachers, this translates into certain luxuries and comforts. To others it means an ability to share and help others. For most, it is a combination of the two.

Just make sure you know what you want your hard-earned money to give you—not just in the long run, but right now. Be an educated consumer!

In pursuit of their financial goals, some teachers—and other professionals—can sometimes forget to cultivate enough interests and passions with which to enjoy the money they eventually accumulate. Make sure, along your financial journey, that you don't neglect to learn (and this *is* something that has to be learned) how to spend your leisure time. Money may seem worthless unless you can enjoy it—now as well as later.

Alan Jay Weiss received his Master of Arts degree from the University of Florida in 1971. His 17 years of experience in the financial services industry include corporate consulting, insurance company management, journal article writing, and the conducting of informational seminars for groups of educators. He currently maintains a financial planning practice for over 1,000 teachers in both Santa Monica, California and Boca Raton, Florida.

Larry Strauss is a freelance writer. He is the co-author of *Growing Younger, When You Have Chest Pains, What Do You Mean You Don't Want to Go to College?* and *Diets That Work.*